Michael Morwood

IT'S TIME

CHALLENGES
to the
DOCTRINE
of the
FAITH

Kelmor Publicati ons
www.kelmorpublishing.com

Scripture quotati ons are from the Common English Bible (CEB). Holy Bible with Apocrypha. 2010

Cover photo:
Crab Nebula, M1, NGC 1952
A composite image of the Crab Nebula showing the X-ray (blue), and opti cal (red) images superimposed.
Credits for X-ray Image:NASA/CXC/ASU/J. Hester et al.
Credits for Opti cal Image: NASA/HST/ASU/J. Hester et al.

IT'S TIME

CHALLENGES
to the
DOCTRINE
of the
FAITH

CONTENTS

INTRODUCTION

The Vatican Curia has nine Congregations responsible for the governance of the Roman Catholic Church. The oldest is the Congregation for the Doctrine of the Faith which Pope Paul III founded in 1542 as the Sacred Congregation of the Universal Inquisition. In 1908, Pope Pius X changed the name to the Sacred Congregation of the Holy Office. It received its present name from Pope Paul VI in 1965.

The Apostolic Constitution on the Roman Curia, *Pastor Bonus*, issued by Pope John Paul II in 1998 states:

> The duty proper to the Congregation for the Doctrine of the Faith is to promote and safeguard the doctrine on faith and morals throughout the Catholic world: for this reason everything which in any way touches such matter falls within its competence. (#48)

For four hundred and seventy years the Congregation for the Doctrine of the Faith (hereafter referred to as the CDF) has exercised unquestioned authority and power in its defense of the faith. This supreme power continues to the present day. Roman

Catholic academics know they cannot publicly question or dissent from what the CDF maintains is acceptable teaching and hope to retain their teaching positions in Roman Catholic institutions or not be denounced as unfaithful to the Church.

In Australia, Bishop William Morris was removed from his diocese in 2011 because the CDF objected to his willingness to ordain women if ever the Church deemed it permissible. In 2012, the Leadership of Catholic Women Religious (LCWR) in the USA came under scrutiny and criticism from the CDF for a perceived lack of fidelity to official Church teaching. In October, 2012, the CDF canonically dismissed Father Roy Bourgeois from the priesthood and from the Maryknoll Fathers and Brothers because of his open support for the ordination of women in the Catholic Church. The same month, the National Catholic Register website carried a statement from the newly appointed head of the CDF, Archbishop Gerhard Müller, directed at the LCWR and anyone inclined to question Rome's teaching authority:

> It is important to remember that at no time in the history of the Church has a group or a movement in one country ever been successful when it has taken an attitude against Rome, when it has been "anti-Rome". Setting oneself up against "Rome" has never brought authentic reform or renewal to the Church. Only through a renewed commitment to the full teaching of Christ and his Church, and through a renewed spirit of

collaboration with the Holy Father and the bishops in communion with him, will there be renewal and new life in the Catholic Church and a new evangelization of our society.

It's Time raises a fundamental question: What if the doctrine being safeguarded by the CDF on behalf of Rome is flawed or is simply not believed anymore by many in the Church, including its own scholars? There is no avenue in the Roman Catholic Church for open dialogue about this serious question. Doctrine is considered a closed book to which everyone must give unquestioning assent. Archbishop Müller indicates clearly that any questioning of doctrine is "anti-Rome". The only way to avoid being "anti-Rome" is to give commitment to the full teaching of "the Church" and agreement with the Pope and the bishops.

However, the questions and the data that suggest the need for a comprehensive examination of the origins and relevance of many doctrines will not go away. If anything, they are increasing and are begging for a forum in which they might be openly and honestly discussed.

The thesis of this book is that much of Catholic doctrine, specifically defined dogma about God, Jesus and Mary, being safeguarded and promoted by the CDF on behalf of the Roman Catholic Church has outlived its use-by date. Most doctrines stem from the Christology, the understanding of "the Christ", promoted by Paul in the pre-scientific religious worldview of two thousand years ago. This worldview cannot be held up to the modern world as a credible picture of reality. Consequently we have a crisis of faith, a crisis that is made worse by the CDF's demand that no questions are to be raised about doctrines expounded in and dependent on a pre-scientific understanding of God, the cosmos and human origins.

It's Time will examine how and why the Roman Catholic Church, through the CDF, has locked itself into a narrow understanding of revelation and faith. It will demonstrate how institutional investment in a closed theology about God and Jesus that gives the Church its unique identity overshadows any openness to scriptural scholarship and to scientific data about this universe.

Our contemporary understanding of the universe, its age, size and development, is vastly different from anything Paul could have imagined when he shaped his Christology. *It's Time* will use this contemporary understanding to articulate faith in God, not as a heavenly deity, but as a Divine Presence permeating and expressing itself in the patterns of operation discernible in the unfolding of the universe and in the development of life on earth. There are undeniable implications for and challenges to traditional doctrine when the notion of God as a heavenly deity is replaced by an understanding that the word "God" points to a Mystery that permeates everything that exists.

If the Divine Presence operates today as a pervasive Presence in the universe, then this must be how the Divine Presence has always revealed itself. This understanding leads us to reflect on Judaism as a religious movement which gave expression to the Divine at work *in* the human endeavor. It was not a movement directed by a God in the heavens. In Judaism, as elsewhere, we see the Divine patterns of operation being expressed in humanity through co-operation, through working together, through sharing and tolerance rather than through violence and domination. We see the message that "salvation" for humanity is linked to living in harmony with and respect for one another. Judaism has always been concerned with *this* world and an awareness of the Divine Presence with people in all they do.

Jesus emerged from the Divine Presence at work *in* the universe, *on* this planet and *in* his Jewish religion. Jesus revealed the Divine within the human. His dream was for people to see the Divine within them so that they would establish "the reign of God" here on earth. His focus was on this world, this life, and how we must give the best possible human expression to the Divine here, now.

Roman Catholic Christology is founded on Paul's understanding of a God in heaven who chose to disconnect from sinful humanity. This is despite the fact that Jesus did not preach about a separation between God and humanity. Nor did he preach about a God who withheld forgiveness.

Paul's ideas radically changed Christianity's understanding not only of Jesus' role, but of Jesus himself. They became the basis for the belief that Jesus had to have a divine nature and be "consubstantial with the Father" in order to gain access to heaven. This doctrine suited an institution that came to believe it had exclusive access to God through Jesus. However, it came at the expense of transforming Jesus into something he never claimed to be (despite what the Gospels suggest), and never needed to be in order to fulfill the role he set for himself.

Doctrine arising from Paul's Christology requires Jesus to have a divine will always in control over his human will. We will see that this theological requisite undermines the heart of Christian spirituality - a genuine response to the invitation of Jesus to know him as a friend who can help ease the burdens of life. It is difficult to be friends with someone who has no experience of the pain and struggle to be good and loving and faithful and of having to search for answers.

It is in rediscovering Jesus, human like us, that Christianity, and Roman Catholicism in particular, could rediscover its true identity and role. This is the Jesus who most clearly reveals the Divine Presence, not only in himself, but in all of us. This is the Jesus who is concerned about this world, who affirms the Divine Presence in us, and who challenges us to give expression to this Presence in all spheres of human activity. It is this Jesus and his life-giving message that should ground "the faith", not "the Christ" of Paul with its focus on gaining access to heaven and winning God's forgiveness. Faith should not rely on or be judged by belief in a God who disconnected himself from humanity, or on whom Jesus had to be in order to reconnect humans with the Divine.

It is time to rediscover what Christian, Catholic "faith" is really about.

1

....

DOCTRINE AND FAITH

"Doctrine" is a generic term covering the teachings of the Church.

Some doctrines have a higher ranking because the Church through the solemn judgment of either a Council or the Pope acting in union with the bishops proposes them to be, in the words of the CDF, "divinely and formally revealed and, as such, as irreformable."

The Church's defense of some doctrines being irreformable is built on the following premises:

Scripture cannot lie. It is God's Word.

Scripture reveals Jesus as God incarnate.

The Church is founded by God Himself.

God sent His Spirit to guide the Church.

The Church therefore cannot err in its solemn doctrinal pronouncements.

The following passages from the *Catechism of the Catholic Church* present the Church's reasoning:

> To compose the sacred books, God chose certain men who, all the while he employed them in this task, made full use of their own faculties and powers so that, though he acted in them and by them, it was as true authors that they consigned to writing whatever he wanted written, and no more. (#106)

> All that has been said about the manner of interpreting Scripture is ultimately subject to the judgement of the Church which exercises the divinely conferred commission and ministry of watching over and interpreting the Word of God. (#119)

> Faith is *certain*. It is more certain than all human knowledge because it is founded on the very word of God who cannot lie. To be sure, revealed truths can seem obscure to human reason and experience, but the certainty that the divine light gives is greater than that which the light of natural reason gives. (#157)

Consider the notion of God used in the *Catechism* for establishing doctrine. The passages call for belief in a male deity who plans, dictates from heaven and ensures the writers write exactly "whatever he wanted written, and no more". Is this a fitting notion of God on which to ground religious faith in the twenty-first century?

Consider also the absolute power Church authority gives itself in regard to interpreting scripture. We are to believe that the power comes from a "divinely conferred commission". Divinely conferred? To what extent is this "commission" dependent on anything Jesus actually said or did? To what extent is it dependent, rather, on the influence of Paul's Christology on the gospel writers?

The *Catechism*, faithfully representing the thinking of the CDF, uses the notion of God as a male deity dictating from the heavens to conclude that since this God cannot lie, doctrine based on Scripture and on this God guiding His Church has to be the most certain of all knowledge.

In its 1998 Doctrinal Commentary on the *Profession of Faith*, the CDF listed the following as irreformable doctrine, known as dogma:

- the articles of faith of the Creed,

- the various Christological dogmas,

- Marian dogmas,

- the doctrine of the institution of the sacraments by Christ and their efficacy with regard to grace,

- the doctrine of the real and substantial presence of Christ in the Eucharist,

- the sacrificial nature of the eucharistic celebration,

- the foundation of the Church by the will of Christ,

- the doctrine on the primacy and infallibility of the Roman Pontiff,

- the doctrine on the existence of original sin,

- the absence of error in the inspired sacred texts,

- the doctrine on the immortality of the spiritual soul and on the immediate recompense after death,

- the doctrine on the grave immorality of direct and voluntary killing of an innocent human being.

The Commentary states:

> These doctrines require the assent of theological faith by all members of the faithful. Thus, whoever obstinately places them in doubt or denies them falls under the censure of heresy, as indicated by the respective canons of the Codes of Canon Law.

The CDF's demand for assent leaves no room whatever for discussion about the notion of God that underpins most of these dogmas and other doctrines.

The next level of doctrine consists of what has been "definitively proposed by the Church regarding teaching on faith". The Commentary states these "are necessary for faithfully keeping and expounding the deposit of faith, even if they have not been proposed by the Magisterium of the Church as formally revealed." An example given is the Church's teaching that only men can be candidates for priestly ordination.

With regard to this level of doctrine, the Commentary states:

> Whoever denies these truths would be in a position of rejecting a truth of Catholic doctrine and would therefore no longer be in full communion with the Catholic Church.

According to Canon Law (833, 5-8) men and women undertaking the following positions must make the *Profession of Faith,* usually at the beginning of their term of office: vicars general, episcopal vicars and judicial vicars; pastors, the rector of a seminary, professors of theology and philosophy in seminaries; those to be promoted to the diaconate, the rectors of an ecclesiastical or Catholic university, teachers in any universities who teach disciplines which deal with faith or morals, and newly appointed superiors in clerical religious institutes and societies of apostolic life.

The *Profession of Faith* consists of the Creed and the following paragraphs that the CDF considers cover assent to the two types of doctrines mentioned above:

In fulfilling the charge entrusted to me in the name of the Church, I shall hold fast to the deposit of faith in its entirety; I shall faithfully hand it on and explain it, and I shall avoid any teachings contrary to it.

I shall follow and foster the common discipline of the entire Church and I shall maintain the observance of all ecclesiastical laws, especially those contained in the Code of Canon Law.

With Christian obedience I shall follow what the Bishops, as authentic doctors and teachers of the faith, declare, or what they, as those who govern the Church, establish. I shall also faithfully assist the diocesan Bishops, so that the apostolic activity, exercised in the name and by mandate of the Church, may be carried out in communion with the Church.

So help me God, and God's Holy Gospels on which I place my hand.

Some bishops are now demanding this Profession of Faith be made by anyone teaching religion in Catholic elementary and high schools or Sunday classes for children.

By requiring the *Profession of Faith*, the CDF ensures that everyone involved in teaching or leadership roles in the Church give their solemn assent to all teaching included in the two levels of doctrine. It is presumed, though unstated, that everyone making the *Profession of Faith* will not question or call into doubt anything contained in what is generally called "the deposit of faith". This effectively forecloses any possibility of open and intellectually rigorous exploration of the worldview or the notion of God that grounds these doctrines. Any attempt to make faith relevant to the world today must be done only within the narrow parameters in which doctrines were shaped. This has led to the untenable situation that educators in faith must ignore the theological implications raised by both the emerging and widely embraced story of the universe, and by the Church's own scriptural scholarship.

Vatican II successfully opened the Catholic Church to engagement with the modern world. The pace of institutional engagement, however, has slowed down considerably in recent decades. One of the main reasons for this has been the desire of Church leadership to protect doctrine from scrutiny or questioning from Catholics' engagement with the information the modern world presents about the universe and how life developed on this planet. This engagement has led people to expand their notion of "God" well beyond the Scriptural notion of a deity in the heavens. It has led people to question doctrine based on belief that the human species emerged into a state of paradise.

While many Roman Catholics at all levels of the church were willing to move into a renewal of faith resonant with their everyday knowledge about the world in which they lived, the Vatican resisted the movement and counteracted. Through the CDF, it reiterated that doctrine cannot be questioned. It insisted that the notion of God underpinning doctrine must not be questioned, and that the worldview in which doctrine was shaped cannot be raised as a reason for questioning doctrine.

Today at one level of faith, there are many Roman Catholics who want to engage the modern world and its scholarship and data, and want their faith to sit reasonably with this new knowledge. These Catholics are interested in exploring questions such as: What is the notion of "God" that will underpin our faith discussions? What is the worldview in which we will situate our understanding of important aspects of faith?

On another level of faith, the CDF and other Roman Catholics resist and ignore any information that differs from the notion of God, the understanding of Scripture, or the worldview in which the Church shaped its doctrinal statements. Doctrine is paramount and beyond questioning.

The *Catechism of the Catholic Church* asserts that "the word of God cannot lie". No one wants to maintain that Scripture "lies". Rather, it is a matter of acknowledging that the scriptural writers inevitably saw and interpreted reality through the worldview of their day. Scholars know that the writers, such as Paul, had to deal with the religious questions that arose from the prevailing worldview. The inflexible approach of the CDF to doctrine, though, is intended to prevent anyone from raising questions about where Paul got his ideas from or asking how the worldview of his day influenced his understanding of "the Christ". Declaring with certainty that a writer like Paul was consigned by God to write God's thoughts conveniently puts Paul's Christology and all Church doctrine dependent on it beyond questioning.

The greatest problem with doctrinal "truth" is that so much of it was shaped in and continues to depend on belief in a heavenly God who denied access to Himself. When belief in this imagination about God and the worldview in which it is encased are questioned, Church leadership appears unable to deal with the challenge. Consequently, it employs the tactic that has worked well over the centuries: it exercises control over thinking at all levels of Church life. It makes unquestioning acceptance of its doctrines a test of loyalty or fidelity to the Church, ensuring there is no public questioning of doctrine.

The *Catechism of the Catholic Church,* which enshrines the outdated theology of revelation and salvation espoused by the CDF is a major component of the tactic. It is commonly used as a tool to stifle any thinking not in accord with the theology that guarantees institutional control over what people are expected to believe.

Under the past two popes, the appointment of "Catechism men" to the office of bishop has further strengthened the tight rein of control over Catholic scholars. In order to silence scholars or refuse to allow speakers in their diocese a bishop need only declare that the scholar or speaker is not in accord with this or that paragraph of the *Catechism.* No intellectual prowess is required by the bishop. All he needs to know is which paragraph of the *Catechism* to cite and to declare that this person is not in accord with the teachings of the Church. It is easy. It is safe. It protects the Church against dangerous thinkers. No dialogue or discussion is allowed. The system of control is intellectually sterile and an embarrassment to Roman Catholicism in its public pronouncements about engaging the modern world.

This ecclesial system of control over thought expects Roman Catholic scholars to believe and to teach concepts such as the following:

- the human species emerged into a state of paradise,

- the sin of the first humans resulted in disconnection from a heavenly God,

- God in heaven conceived a plan of salvation to restore humans to favor,

- Jesus is the incarnate son of a God who came down from the heavens,

- Jesus knew he was God incarnate,

- Jesus died to ensure God's forgiveness for human sin,

- only through Jesus the Christ is divine life accessible to humanity,

- Jesus' death was necessary in order for God to grant access to Himself in heaven,

- Jesus set up a new religion. This new religion began at Pentecost.

- the Spirit of God only came down upon earth after Jesus was taken up into heaven,

- the only sacred writings inspired by the "Holy Spirit" are "the canonical books of the Old and new Testaments." (#8 *Dominus Iesus,* a Declaration released by the CDF in 2000)

- "Above all else, it must be firmly believed that the Church, a pilgrim now on earth, is necessary for salvation ...God has willed that the Church founded by Jesus Christ be the instrument for the salvation of humanity..." (*#20-21 Dominus Iesus*)

It is time to question seriously the basis of such "truths". For example,

Is "God" *really* a heavenly deity who withheld graciousness and forgiveness?

Is it possible to be *really* disconnected from "God"?

Did the human species *really* emerge into a state of paradise?

Did Jesus *really* believe in a God who withheld forgiveness and denied access to "Himself"?

Did Jesus *really* think the Spirit of God was not intimately present in the everyday lives of people of his time?

Did Jesus *really* renounce his Judaism and start a new religion?

Did Jesus *really* ordain anyone?

Did Jesus *really* ascend physically into the heavens?

Was Pentecost *really* the birthday of a new religion?

Did Paul *really* die as a member of a new religion distinct from Judaism?

The CDF, however, will not entertain such troubling questions or the data and the scholarship associated with them. Instead, it uses doctrines, shaped in the worldview of two thousand years ago, as absolute truths never to be questioned and demands a "Yes, I believe" response to each of them. There is no possibility of dialogue about how and why a particular doctrine emerged in the first place.

The questions must be examined and the dialogue encouraged if the Catholic Church is to be relevant to the modern world. Unfortunately for the Church, the CDF and the majority of bishops are not capable of engaging the questions or participating in a scholarly dialogue. Instead, they choose to stay enclosed within the framework of theology that does not and cannot engage the reality of the world as we know it today.

It is time to break from the worldview of two thousand years ago with its notions of a Supreme overlord God who lived in the heavens and who disconnected access to "Himself" because of some supposed sin by the first human. It is time to question the Christology that is tied to that outdated worldview and interprets the importance of Jesus - and the institutional Church - in terms of unique access to that heavenly deity.

It is time to do what the Second Vatican Council did not do: explore the notion of "God" that fits with what we know today about the universe.

It is time to look anew at how the reality of "God" manifests itself and comes to expression throughout the universe through "patterns of operation". It is time to look and see how these patterns of the Divine Presence at work are manifested in the slow development of life on earth and in the unfolding of the human species.

It is time to look and see, and to really grasp the truth that the Divine has been, is, and always will be *here* and *everywhere*. It is time to rid ourselves of the notion, canonized in our Scriptures, in traditional Christology, in the Creed, in doctrines and in the Magisterium's claim to represent God on earth, that "God" is essentially a heavenly deity who disconnected "Himself" from the human species.

It is time to take seriously that the Reality Underpinning All That Exists is not a god, not even a God, ruling from the heavens.

This Fundamental Reality that underpins and holds everything in existence is everywhere. It is a Presence, *Divine* because it is the source of everything, always active, never absent, and so makes everything sacred.

It is time to return to what we all learnt and knew instinctively as children - before we were locked into scriptural and Church stories about a God who lived in heaven and locked us out - that this Divine Presence is in every breath we take, in every atom, in every flower, in every person. We live in a universe permeated with the Breath, the Spirit of this Presence.

It is time to look again at the basics of Christian faith, but now we do so, not with the idea or the belief that God is a heavenly deity, but with the belief that the Divine Presence has been, is, and always will be, the Energizing, Sustaining, Everywhere, Reality creatively present on earth, deep within all of us, seeking the best possible expression that it can attain in human form.

2

....

THE DIVINE PRESENCE

To what do we think we are referring when we use the word "God" in the twenty first century?

Many Christians reject the traditional notion of "God". They do so from an understanding that belief in "God" as an elsewhere, overseeing Lord of the universe does not fit anymore. It is too tied to images of earth as the center of the universe and of heaven as God's dwelling place above the earth, and to the up-down language associated with those images.

It is time to take seriously what Christianity has always proclaimed: that this Mysterious Presence we call "God" is everywhere and it is beyond all our human concepts. It is time to make a significant shift in our understanding of "God". It is time to shift from notions of a deity to an understanding and appreciation of the Divine Presence always here, always and everywhere active in an expanding universe and in the evolution of life on this planet.

Institutional religion's resistance to this shift is understandable because it has significant investment in the notion of an
elsewhere deity. That notion of God underpins the Creed and
Church doctrines about God, about Jesus and about humanity's
relationship with God. It is the notion of God on which Church
authority depends to justify the claim that it has unique access
to God through the resurrection of Jesus. It is the notion of God
in our scriptures: a heavenly deity who reacts, plans, has definite
opinions, intervenes, controls, and sends His Son from heaven
to earth. It is the notion of God that Church leadership uses to
claim that its authority stems from a "divinely conferred commission". It is the notion of God that Church leadership relies
on in its claim to know the express views of God on important
issues.

While the resistance is understandable, it is lamentable.
Christianity has traditionally proclaimed belief in the *everywhere* presence of God, an everywhere Presence holding and
sustaining everything in existence. The shift being proposed
here is rooted in fidelity to this belief, in being ready to explore
its implications for Christian faith, and most importantly, in
the desire to understand the person and message of Jesus in the
light of what we know today about our universe, rather than the
worldview of two thousand years ago.

The shift starts with considering the age and size of the universe
in which we live, and with what it means to say that the Divine
Presence is everywhere, holding and sustaining everything in

existence. What does it mean to believe that there is no outside of this Presence? And how can we best discern this Mystery present and active in everything that exists?

If this Presence is everywhere, "charging" and holding everything in existence, we should be able to discern the Presence through examining how the universe unfolds. It makes eminent sense, then, to go to the scientific world and discover the basic, universal patterns of operation in the emergence and expansion of the universe and in the development of life on earth. These patterns of operation can and should be our contemporary pointers to the Presence. They will point us well beyond the "God" of scripture and doctrine to an awesome Mystery in which we live and move and to which we give human expression.

What is the "big picture" contemporary science paints for us about how the universe expands and develops that would help us discern and appreciate the Divine Presence through all and in all?

One of the major scientific developments in recent decades is the shift from understanding the world around us in purely physical or material terms, as if everything from atoms to galaxies operated like machines and that everything could be reduced to its working parts. Those of us who are older will remember studying physics in school. It was all rather simple: a case of learning what went with what, and knowing the laws explaining the how and why of what happened.

Nowadays science finds itself speaking in terms of mystery and wonder as it tries to explain the how and why of reality. How and why, at the deepest level of matter, particles get together with other particles to form atoms, atoms get together with other atoms to form molecules, molecules get together and form single cells, and single cells get together and form multi-cellular life. How, for example, do sixty trillion cells in our bodies know what to do? How do some cells in an embryo "know" to form a set of ears, and other cells produce a heart and other cells produce kidneys?

These processes of development can no longer be adequately explained in purely physical terms, as if this goes with that and that goes with this and look what happens. Science acknowledges something deeper within the very fabric of matter, something that is more than matter. Energy is working in tune with some organizing principle that is not physical. Scientists refer to this as "consciousness" or "mind" operating at every level of matter. This is not the consciously aware "mind" that we humans exercise, but mind/consciousness that is an essential aspect of physical reality itself.

Energy does not think. Consciousness does not think. A particle does not think, an atom does not think. The cells in our bodies do not think. The universe expands and develops in ways of relating and acting that make our human mode of thinking and acting slow and cumbersome in comparison.

As we study the unfolding of matter throughout the universe and study the development of life on this planet, it seems there is inbuilt into matter the capacity to co-operate with other entities in order to produce something beyond each of the entities. Cells have the capacity to organize themselves, to maintain and repair themselves, to store and remember information and to call upon it when needed, and to work in harmony with other cells to produce the wonders of a flower, a bird, the human body. There is an inbuilt system of intentionality in the constant movement to development, to produce something beyond the co-operating cells themselves. And there is no thinking involved in this process, not the way we humans experience thinking. Each of sixty trillion cells in our bodies produces 10,000 bio-electro-chemical reactions *every second*. The reactions need to be almost instantly correlated and set in motion. Our bodies would surely be in a mess if each cell had to stop and think about what it needed to do.

This capacity to self-organize and to work in relationship with other entities is universal. Without it, the universe could not have produced galaxies or stars or planets or life on earth. Here, on earth, the same pattern is the driving force of evolution. Scientists insist that co-operation, not survival of the fittest or domination, is the key pattern in the emergence of life.

Let us explore how this basic information might shape our understanding of "God" as a universal Presence underpinning all that has ever existed.

If we take seriously that energy and consciousness are all-pervasive and woven into the very fabric of reality then this knowledge could be the best means we have for a deeper understanding or appreciation that the Divine Presence is everywhere. This is not to suggest in any way that the Divine Presence can be reduced to energy or consciousness. Rather, the information helps us to appreciate universality on a grand scale. When we recognize patterns operating on such a vast scale, we can use these patterns as contemporary pointers to the Divine present and active always and everywhere in the universe. This is not some sort of pantheism. The Divine Presence is more than the universe or the world around us and far more than anything we can comprehend in human notions.

An appreciation of the universality of the Divine Presence challenges us to move from the traditional understanding of "God" as a divine Super Person who thinks, reacts, needs to be worshipped, keeps a record of wrongs, withholds forgiveness and access to "Himself", and rules over the world. Most of us were so steeped from early childhood in the imagination and belief about "God" as a deity in heaven that we failed as adults to stop and think about what we are imagining and from where this imagination came. We were taught to pray to a "God" who thinks about whether to respond. We learned a creed about a "God" who lives somewhere else and sent his son down to us. We were never educated to question the images on which these concepts were based.

It is time to move on from belief in a heavenly God whose thinking and actions mirror our rather primitive human way of thinking and acting. We humans regard our conscious awareness, our capacity for reflective thinking, as the greatest by-product of the universe. We have consistently transferred our way of thinking onto a God, as if by having a God who thinks and loves and acts as we do, we are somehow expanding our appreciation of the Divine Presence. In fact, what we are doing is limiting our understanding and appreciation of the Presence as Mystery. It is time to stop telling a story about a God in heaven who did this and that, and who thinks this and that. The awesome, mysterious, Divine Presence is far beyond all that.

In one sense, there is nothing new in what is being said here because Christianity has always proclaimed that "God is everywhere". What is new is the scientific data we have as pointers to the Divine Presence all around us. Attention to the way energy and consciousness operate throughout the universe can lead to a deeper faith perspective that enables us to appreciate that everything around us is "charged" with the Divine Presence. We can have a heightened sense, a clearer conscious awareness, that the universe pulsates with, gives expression to, the Divine Presence.

Thousands of years ago, humans had a sense of this Presence all around them. Then, a major shift occurred. Formal religion took this Presence from the earth and placed it in the heavens in the form of gods. Later development in religious thinking led the

Hebrew people to imagining and believing there was only one god, an Almighty God who ruled from above.

It is surely ironic that formal religion brought the "original sin" to the world. It removed the Divine from earth and placed it in the heavens. It was formal religion that separated humanity from a previously intimate and profound sense of the Divine here on earth. It was formal religion that led people into images and notions about exile from God. It was formal religion that told people they were basically sinful and that only adherence to a particular religion could bring them "salvation", as long as they dutifully obeyed the teachings and practices of that religion.

Formal religion took its mind and eyes and heart off the here and now and focused instead on notions of separation and on the need for mediators and priests with special powers to access the heavenly God. Formal religion established systems that made people dependent on middle-managers who could access God for them and tell them, with unquestioned authority, what God's thoughts were on almost every aspect of community life.

And all the while, the Creative, Divine, Energizing Reality, this incredible Presence that brought the universe into being, was really here on earth, being expressed in peoples' lives. The Presence did not and could not move from here. Only formal religion could make people believe otherwise.

There is a widespread shift in consciousness among people today, a shift that reflects and gives expression to the Divine

Presence embedded in everything that exists. It is about people breaking free of religious images and creeds and beliefs that lock them into thinking the "next life" is what really matters. It is the growing awareness that "salvation" for the world is not about access to a heavenly God. It is about being attentive to how the Divine Presence is expressed in the human endeavor and how, in the words of Jesus, we are to make "the kingdom of God" evident in the human community.

It is time to tell a different story of human relationship with the Divine. Our starting point will be the religion of Jesus, Judaism, and how it sought to give clear expression to the Divine Presence at work in the human community.

3

....

THE DIVINE PRESENCE AND JUDAISM

Our contemporary appreciation of the universality of the Divine Presence provides a new context in which to understand the origins, development and central message of the Jewish religion. The message does not change, but the context differs significantly from the traditional Jewish understanding that a God in the heavens chose a poor, downtrodden ethnic group to enter into covenant with Him and be His chosen people. It also differs considerably from the traditional Christian understanding that a God in heaven chose the Jewish people to be His people for the purpose of preparing the world for the coming of His Son who would repair the disconnection caused by the sin of the first humans.

In the context of the Divine Presence always here, always active in all human affairs, we can look back and see how the Jewish people used the worldview of the time to interpret their relationship with their God. They imagined a God in heaven was organizing events here on earth. But now our worldview is different. Our context is different. Our understanding is different. Our appreciation of the Divine Presence being always here on earth within and among all people is heightened. We understand that this Presence does not operate from the heavens down, but from *within* and *among* the human community. It is a Presence writ deep into the human psyche, as it is written deep into every particle and atom and cell. This being so, we should expect to find this Presence given voice in men and women all around the world expressing how humanity can live in harmony with this Presence and give the best possible human expression to it. Indigenous spiritualties, matriarchal societies, innumerable religious movements, the Buddha, Confucius, and many other individuals gave voice to the Presence.

When we look back to the origins of Judaism and to its message we see this Presence given voice and human expression in accord with the same patterns of operation we see everywhere in the universe. It is a voice, a call, from deep within the human that cries out for humans to work together, to be sensitive to one another, to overcome selfishness, to stop the violence, to care, to build up, to work in harmony with all of creation, and to entertain possibilities for the human endeavor way beyond what we presently experience.

Humanity is capable of destroying itself and everything around it when it blocks this expression of the Divine. Humanity can give its best expression to the Divine only when it frees itself from destructive activity and behavior that demean and hurt other people and damages the natural world. Humans can only truly experience and give expression to the Divine Presence within them when they follow the universal life-giving patterns of co-operation and working together.

The Hebrew prophets did hear, as they inevitably expressed it, "the voice of the Lord saying to me..." But in reality it was not a voice from heaven breaking through to them in their dreams or visions or enlightened moments. No, it was the impulse, the "voice", of the Divine Presence within the human breaking out into clear expression. It is time to move our understanding of "revelation" beyond the notion of a deity in heaven dictating how humanity should live.

This "voice", or movement of the Divine within Judaism, was not concerned with the "next life" or with a God who had disconnected from humans. Rather, this consistent, prophetical voice addressed the very identity and role of the Jewish people: they were to create a society that would be a "light to the nations". Other peoples would see in this community what society looked like when people lived acutely conscious of the call to give religious, social, economic and political expression to the belief that the Divine Presence was embedded in their existence and conduct.

We need to look at the prophetical movement within Judaism with a renewed understanding that the prophets gave expression to the Divine Presence within them when they preached: *This is what humans must do to give proper expression to the Divine*, or, as they expressed it, in their understanding of a heavenly God speaking through them: *This is what God wants*.

So what did the Divine Presence coming to clear expression within the Jewish prophetical movement ask of humanity?

In well-known scripture texts we hear how the Divine Presence will be known and experienced here on earth. It is through life-affirming human behavior that we will recognize that "God dwells with us", that we are "walking in God's paths" and that this is "the path to salvation". Salvation is about saving ourselves from the misery we humans inflict on ourselves.

> If you truly reform your ways and your actions; if you treat each other justly; if you stop taking advantage of the immigrant orphan, or widow; if you don't shed the blood of the innocent in this place, or go after other gods to your own ruin, only then will I dwell with you in this place. (Jeremiah 7:5-7)

Today, we should read a text such as this not in terms of a God in heaven dictating to Jeremiah the conditions for God's presence on earth. Rather, we should read it as the Divine Presence within Jeremiah enlightening him to understand: *if we act this way, then we will experience the Divine Presence within and among us*. We have to turn our understanding of "revelation" upside down from the traditional understanding of an elsewhere deity speaking through his chosen messengers and having them write "whatever he wanted written and no more".

In Hosea a similar insight surfaced, one that should be the heart and soul of any religion:

> I desire faithful love and not sacrifice, the knowledge
> of God instead of entirely burned offerings. (6:6)

Hosea knew instinctively, as we all do, that living lovingly gives the best human expression to the Divine. He was telling us something we all know in the depths of our being.

As with all the prophets, Micah presented his message in terms of God speaking, but it is time to hear the message not as one coming from heaven down to us but as one rising from the Divine Presence actively expressing itself in and through the human community:

> He has told you, human one, what is good; and what
> the Lord requires of you: to do justice, embrace faithful
> love, and walk humbly with your God. (6:8)

The reality here is that we humans *know* "what is good". We do not need and should not expect to be told by an external deity what is good. The knowledge is implanted deep within us. The Divine Presence is within all of us.

The Divine Presence has always been in the development of the human species, yet humanity has been consistent in ignoring the promptings to goodness, decency and compassion, turning instead to selfishness, oppression, greed, false securities, competition, pride and domination. Humanity needs to hear the voice within all of us saying: "Act justly and do what is righteous because my salvation is coming soon and my righteousness will be revealed." (Isaiah 56:1) "My salvation", God's salvation, is really our salvation from the damage we do to ourselves. There is only one way to achieve it, and it is not through military might or economic greed or a gospel of prosperity. No, Isaiah gave voice to what is necessary for us to do. We are to achieve it by:

> … releasing wicked restraints, untying the ropes of a yoke, setting free the mistreated…sharing your bread with the hungry and bringing the homeless poor into your house, covering the naked when you see them, and not hiding from your own family.

Then,

> Your light will break out like the dawn and you will be healed quickly. Your own righteousness will walk before you and the Lord's glory will be your rear guard…If you open your heart to the hungry, and provide abundantly for those who are afflicted, your light will shine in the darkness and your gloom will be like the noon. (58:6-8,10)

The Hebrew Bible, in stark contrast to the way in which nations and societies operate, and against all the ambitions of powerful and rich people, makes clear that *only* when such a social agenda is put in place will:

> The sun will no longer be your light by day… the Lord will be your everlasting light and your days of mourning will be ended. (Isaiah 60:19-20)

And:

> Many nations will go and say, "Come, let's go … to the house of Jacob's God so that he may teach us his ways and we may walk in God's paths." (Isaiah 2:2-3)

The time has come for Christianity to honor and admire this "call" within Judaism and to restore it to its rightful place when Christianity explains what inspired Jesus of Nazareth, and what it thinks Jesus was trying to do in his public ministry. The obvious lesson from Jesus' Jewish background is that the Divine Presence at work in the human community was, is and always will be *primarily concerned with life on earth*.

If we do not place Jesus in this prophetical tradition with Judaism, we will not appreciate the central thrust of his teaching and ministry or what he was prepared to die for. Instead, we will be distracted, as the Christian religion has been for two thousand years, by notions that Jesus was really concerned about getting people into heaven and meeting "God" there, rather than experiencing the Divine Presence here, and making the "kingdom of God" evident here on earth.

It is time to see Jesus and his preaching in the context of the
Divine Presence always here on earth, always active in the
human community as everywhere, rather than in the context of a
heavenly deity manipulating events on earth.

4

JESUS - HUMAN EXPRESSION OF THE DIVINE PRESENCE

There is no evidence that Jesus ever renounced his Jewish religion or asked any of his followers to renounce Judaism. He did not start a new religion. Matthew's Gospel, written some fifty years after Jesus died, has Jesus saying: *"Do not think I have come to abolish the law and the prophets. I have come not to abolish, but to fulfill them."* (5:17) The passage comes immediately after Jesus urges his listeners to be the salt of the earth and the light of the world. How are they to do this? They will do it, he says by a "holiness" that "surpasses" the mere keeping of laws. (5:20).

This stance is not unique to Jesus. Indeed, as the author of Matthew's Gospel portrays Jesus, it is thoroughly Jewish, completely faithful to Judaism. There is no indication that the fulfillment Jesus speaks of is to be found in a religion separate from Judaism. No, Jesus was well aware that Jeremiah, Isaiah, Micah,

Hosea and the other prophetical voices throughout Jewish history had expressed the non-negotiable conditions for giving true human expression to the Divine Presence. Jesus knew from his Jewish religion what the "kingdom of God" was about. He knew what it would take to make God's kingdom visible on earth. He knew the mess humanity found itself in. He saw the violence, the fear, the domination, the suppression, the poverty, the discrimination, and the indifference of religious leaders to the authentic expression of Judaism. He also knew that if he spoke against the religious and political power-brokers of his time he would suffer the consequences.

It is time to make this our starting point for reflection on Jesus as the human expression of the Divine Creative Reality that Christians have called "God".

While it is highly likely that Jesus, along with other Jews of his time, thought of God as a male heavenly deity, it is also evident from his preaching about the kingdom of God that he recognized and emphasized the Spirit of God present in people listening to him. His preaching about the kingdom of God and the need to establish it resonates with what we believe today about the Divine Presence permeating everything that exists.

In chapter 61 of the Book of Isaiah, the prophet who preached so earnestly about the reign of God on earth through justice and concern for the poor professes he was "anointed" by God to preach this good news. Clearly, this did not entail a physical anointing. Rather, the prophet understood he was chosen by God to perform a task.

The prophet says:

> The Lord God's spirit is upon me, because the Lord has anointed me. He has sent me to bring good news to the poor, to bind up the brokenhearted; to proclaim release for captives...to comfort those who mourn. (61:1-3)

This same text is put on Jesus' lips early in his ministry (Luke 4:18-19) to express how he saw his role. We should take special note of the word "anointed", which in Greek is "christos". It is from this word that the Christian understanding of "Christ" emerged. It is important to take note of this because "christos" was applied to Jesus in a completely different context and with a very different meaning after he died. Christianity has failed and continues to fail to understand Jesus rightly because our Christian Scriptures, written decades after he died, are dominated by a different perspective about "christos", one that ignored Jesus' own understanding of the task he set for himself.

That later perspective, as we will see, began with the notion that Jesus was taken up into heaven by a God who lived in the heavens. There, in heaven, he was supposedly anointed by God to be the judge of the "living and the dead". According to this thinking, it was in heaven that Jesus became "the Christ" and thereby won God's forgiveness for human sin, won access to

God's dwelling place in heaven for humans, and released "God's Spirit" upon a select group on earth.

Jesus ministry indicates he saw himself as "christos" on the human, prophetical level. This is clear in his constant use of the term "son of man", ("the human one") of himself. What Christianity did very early in its development, as we shall see in the next chapter, was to transform Jesus from the human "christos" into a cosmic figure, a capital C "Christos". This "Christology", articulated so clearly by Paul, subsequently became the lens through which the Gospels were written.

We will set aside this later development for the moment, and focus on Jesus and his concern for the establishment of the "kingdom of God" here on earth. Only when we focus on Jesus, "the human one", who saw himself called by God to preach the good news about the Divine Presence in peoples' lives will we gain a true understanding of the importance of his preaching to humanity then and now.

In our twenty first century perspective of the Divine Presence at work in the universe we can better appreciate Jesus' insight that the Divine was within him and all around him. However, he also realized that people did not "see" what he saw, and because they could not "see" it, there was little hope of changing the way society operated or for changing the sway of military power and economic interests that impoverished people. The people with power, prestige, riches, control and authority were not interested in reforming the social, political, economic and religious conditions that caused the majority of people to be afflicted, brokenhearted and in mourning.

How to bring about change? That was the concern for Jesus. How to bring about a society that would reflect the Divine Presence evident in peoples' lives and their interactions? How to bring about a society that Judaism had long dreamed about and considered itself called to establish?

When we get beneath the classic Christology evident in the Gospels about a God-figure dying for the sins of humanity, we find another story much more realistic and faithful to the situation in which Jesus found himself. That story is the ministry of Jesus as he tried to persuade people to take responsibility, as faithful Jews, to establish "God's reign" on earth, not Caesar's, not Herod's, not that of the rich and powerful, but God's reign. He went to "the crowd", the lowly, the afflicted, the broken hearted, those in mourning, and told them he had good news for them and that with the aid of this good news they could establish the "kingdom of God" on earth.

We need to be clear about this. This is the task Jesus saw himself as fulfilling. He gave his heart and soul to *this task*, to helping people see how they could make visible God's reign on earth.

Jesus' first step with the "crowd" was to clear away attitudes and beliefs and religious practices that prevented people from seeing and experiencing what he believed, that the "Lord God's spirit", the Breath of God, the Divine Presence, was with them. Jesus recognized that unless people came to a profound belief in the Spirit being upon or within them, nothing was going to change. People would continue to expect that only a God in heaven could change the situation. They were nobodies, after all. God could not expect anything of the likes of them. It was this attitude that Jesus had to change.

Jesus set out to "convert", to turn upside down, the way people thought about themselves and about their relationship with God. This was a pre-condition for them to be able or willing to establish "God's reign" on earth. The two key impediments he had to address were peoples' fear of God and their belief that God was not close to them.

Fear of God was part and parcel of the religious worldview that imagined God as a heavenly ruler in charge of everything that happened. In a pre-scientific religious society it was common for people to link sickness, pain, disaster and even one's lowly position in society with God's supreme control over everything. Consequently, when bad things happened, people understood it as punishment from God for some wrongdoing. We can imagine the people who constituted "the crowd" being immersed in this thinking all their lives. As they saw it, the evidence of God's punishment for sin was all around them. If you were part of the crowd you would be looking over your shoulder to see what might be coming your way either from your own misconduct or through the sin of someone else in the family tree. You would hardly consider yourself to be part of God's plan to establish God's reign on earth!

Jesus addressed the fear people had of the God they imagined ruled the world. His call to "conversion" challenged people to think about and change their imagination about God. He invited them to consider relationship with God as akin to the relationship a child would have with a most loving, trusted parent. This is part of the brilliance of Jesus and his teaching. He was not trying to describe God. He was describing a relationship of trust that will stand the test of time, whatever people understand "God" to be.

For Jesus, God was not to be thought of as a deity who withheld mercy and forgiveness. On the contrary, his understanding of God conceived of graciousness beyond measure, beyond all human expectations. His parables, such as the Prodigal Son and the Vineyard Workers, invited people to reflect on and reject any beliefs they had about God keeping a record of wrongs and waiting to dispense punishment as people deserved.

Jesus invited the crowd to step into his perspective and immerse themselves in the understanding that Graciousness Beyond Measure ran the universe, not a punitive God who could not be trusted. If this was the nature of God, then the logical step was for people to free themselves from religious ideas about God inflicting sickness, suffering or impoverishment on them.

Suffering has nothing to do with a God allowing it or wanting it to happen. Some of it stems from the natural world. Some of it is caused by innocent human mistake. Much, if not most of it, is caused by humans acting contrary to goodness, fairness, decency and compassion. We call it evil. Evil is not God's problem. It is ours. We create it. It is a human problem. We create oppression, war, starvation, domination, prejudice, inequality, greed and injustice. We, not a God in heaven, have to overcome evil.

Jesus clearly dissociated himself from any notions of a God who would use suffering to test peoples' loyalty. Jesus would not want people to ask, "Why has God done this to me?" or "Why has God allowed this to happen?" Rather, Jesus invited people into a relationship of utter trust with their God and in the security of that trusting relationship to look for other causes of their suffering, not God.

Closely linked with Jesus' efforts to set people free from fear of God was his desire for people to see and "own" the Presence of the Divine with them in their everyday living and loving. Without people coming to affirm and appreciate this Presence within them nothing could ever change. The movement for extraordinary change could only come from deeply felt convictions in people that the Divine was moving within and among them.

People in the crowd who readily believed that God was not at all close to them would surely have been greatly surprised and puzzled to hear this preacher trying to convert them into believing God was close to them. They must have asked Jesus how they would *know* God was close to them. The simplicity of his approach is startling. He took the events of everyday life and asked people to reflect on, to *name* and *to appreciate* activities they considered to be basically mundane and relatively unimportant, as human expressions of the Divine. He urged people to look and to see more deeply, that when they visited, when they clothed, when they were kind to one another, when they forgave, and when they acted lovingly, that these activities were expressions of the Divine Presence within them. Although there are no long speeches in the Gospels about this, there is a very clear summary of the simplicity of Jesus' preaching and convictions in 1 John 4:7,12: *Everyone who loves is born from God and knows God... If we love each other, God remains in us and his love is made perfect in us.* Jesus wanted people to allow that "knowing" to rise in their minds and hearts. If they could identify the "Spirit of the Lord" within them in with their everyday loving, then both Jesus' and Judaism's dream of establishing the "reign of God" on earth could be achieved.

The experience of love is humanity's best window to the Divine. Love gives the Divine Presence its best possible human expression. Love is linked with graciousness, with creativity, with expansiveness, with sharing, with co-operation, with moving the lover and the beloved beyond selfishness. It is doubtless why some of the greatest Jewish teachers told people to concentrate on just one commandment that can be summed up as, *Love God with everything you have.* It is easy to imagine Jesus steeped in the conviction that love is everything. It is easy to imagine Jesus giving wonderful human expression to graciousness, expansiveness, hope, and forgiveness.

Jesus believed the Spirit of God was with him. He understood that the Divine Presence is an intrinsic aspect of being human and that not only he, but that all people have this Presence within them. Ultimately, it is the expression of this Presence within the human community that will overcome evil and establish a society that will be a light to the nations.

When we grasp this, we are better able to appreciate the challenge confronting us in Jesus' teaching: to give expression to the Divine Presence, Love Itself, in all our social interactions. If the Divine is gracious beyond measure, and if we in our loving give human expression to the Divine at work in us, then it follows that we are to love graciously and generously. We are to be compassionate. We are to be merciful and forgiving. We are to be neighbor to everyone, even to people we consider our enemies. We are to establish "God's way" of acting.

For Jesus, nothing was more important than establishing "the kingdom of God" here on earth. Nothing. This message is the heart and soul of his preaching. Go, sell everything. Do not look back. Do not make excuses. Do not delay. This is the treasure in the field. This is the pearl of great price. Stop worrying about all other issues. Concentrate on this.

It is clear Jesus did not go to the "crowd" and tell people that God had locked them out of heaven or that God was withholding forgiveness and access. It is clear he did not see himself as a mediator between people and a distant God. It is clear that his ministry was motivated by the urgent necessity for the human community to change the way it operated at all levels of society. It is clear that his preaching focused on how people might bring this change about. It is clear, as Matthew's Gospel states, that Jesus saw his purpose in life was to "fulfill" the dream the Divine Presence had expressed in Judaism through the great prophets.

Matthew's Gospel presents the Beatitudes as the way to that fulfillment. The word, beatitude, along with the usual expression, "Blessed are…" can be somewhat misleading. It can give the false impression of comfort or blessing at the expense of the challenge of what is being asked. The beatitudes are not really about blessings, except in a long range view that eventually blessings will come. Rather, the statements should be heard as challenging injunctions. They should be heard as: *you are to do this…*; *you are to live this way.* They are prerequisites for experiencing the Divine Presence within and among us. Only when these conditions are present will people "see God" or have the right to be called "children of God" or know that "the kingdom of heaven" is truly here on earth. Living the challenges of the

Beatitudes is the criterion for anyone who professes to be a follower of Jesus.

The conditions are clear cut: You are not to be proud-hearted or domineering or the cause of anyone's suffering. You are not to separate yourself from the sufferings of others. You are to mourn with people who are suffering. And if you suffer, your comfort is not to be that of self-pity or withdrawal. You are comforted by others who know mourning, so stay in solidarity with them. You are not to use violence, but are to be strong in your resolve. You are to act in accord with the prophetical voice of Judaism; you are to speak up and fight for justice and an end to oppression. You are to be compassionate and merciful, in tune with the minds and hearts of others so that understanding and healing are possible rather than hardline positions that lead to distrust, enmity and wars. You are to be pure in heart; you are not to be distracted by riches, fame or power. You are not to be "bought off" or distracted from purity of intent by aligning yourself with the rich, the powerful, the military, the economic and political rulers of the world. You are not to lord it over people. You are to be neighbor and to be gracious to all as the Divine Presence is gracious to all.

The beatitudes challenge us to be a light that shines and lets everyone know where we stand. They challenge us to stop being anxious and concerned about things that are passing and do not really matter. We are to "Seek first God's kingdom and God's righteousness..." And we should expect ridicule and persecution because this "way" is not the way of the world.

Most importantly, we are to understand that:

> Everybody who hears these words of mine and doesn't
> put them into practice will be like a fool who built a
> house on sand... It fell and was completely destroyed.
> (Matthew 7:26-27)

It is time to understand Jesus as someone "driven" by the Divine Presence *within* him, not by an external God directing him from the heavenly heights to repair lost access to that God.

It is time to understand him as someone who saw what other people either were unable or refused to see: that the Divine Presence was within them.

It is time to see that Jesus wanted people to establish here on earth a way of human interaction that reflected the Divine Presence in all they did.

It is time to appreciate the urgency of Jesus' preaching about the "kingdom of God" and its importance for humanity today.

It is time to explore why, like most of the people who listened to Jesus in his lifetime, institutional Christianity allowed itself to be distracted from the heart of Jesus' teaching. It sold its soul to the empires of the day, and lost all humbleness of mind and heart in its systems of governance and its control over people's thinking.

In significant ways, Roman Catholic leadership does look "foolish" today through its inability to engage the modern world, through its reliance on unquestioning adherence to outmoded doctrines, through intellectual sterility, through its transparent failure to witness to the spirit of the Beatitudes in its handling of sexual abuse victims, and through its repressive control over the Church's own scholarship.

It is time to ask why doctrines about Jesus winning access to heaven became the dominant theology of the Christian religion and how Christianity became so distracted from the basic message of Jesus.

5

....

PAUL'S CHRISTOLOGY

We need to have some appreciation of the twenty year period after Jesus' death if we are to understand the change in thinking that took place in the second half of the first century.

Although we have no documents from the period between the death of Jesus and the appearance of Paul's letters, some scripture scholars conjecture that there may have been a document from this time period that later became a source used by the authors of the gospels of Matthew and Luke. Whether or not such a document existed, it seems that the focus of the Jesus movement in this twenty year period was on the "kingdom of God". The movement gathered around the belief that Jesus, the "son of man", the human one, preached with urgency and intensity the need to establish God's reign on earth. This movement was a way of life and was radical in its embrace of the preaching of Jesus.

It seems highly likely, from what scripture scholarship can ascertain, that in this twenty year period Jesus was considered by members of the movement to be a Jewish prophetical figure. As in the preaching of Jesus, there is no evidence that the movement was concerned with access to the heavenly realms. The concern was to change this world. The focus was on Jesus preaching a way of life that would express the Divine Presence in human living and loving.

It is important to acknowledge that this was a Jewish movement. It was not a new religion. There is no evidence to suggest that any members of the movement thought they were part of a new religion.

There are no written narratives from this time about Jesus' birth; no annunciation story, no virginal conception. There are no resurrection stories.

Then, beginning mid-century with Paul's writings, and culminating in John's gospel at the end of the century, a monumental shift in thinking about Jesus occurred.

We have been distracted from the magnitude of this shift by the story of Pentecost, which we have been led to believe heralded the beginning of the Christian religion fifty days after Easter. Such was not the case, as we shall see in the next chapter. For the time being, let us keep in mind that the first followers of Jesus were Jews. This was a Jewish movement. Paul died a Jew. He never renounced his Judaism. The followers of Jesus did not separate themselves from Judaism until after Paul died.

Paul was a Jew who understood he had a calling from God to expand Judaism by preaching about Jesus to "the gentiles". Many Christians mistakenly believe the gentiles were pagans who had no connection with Judaism. In fact they were non-Jews who had some connection with the Jewish community, had respect for the Jewish way of life and had some knowledge of the Jewish God. It is clear in the Acts of the Apostles, (chapters 13-19), that Paul made contact with the gentiles, sometimes called "the God-fearing", through visiting the Jewish communities and preaching in the synagogues. Paul sought to bring these people into full participation in the Jewish community. He did not intend to lay the foundations of a new religion separate from Judaism. This is another historical fact unknown to many Christians.

Acts 13:13-15 describes Paul going to Antioch in Pisidia. On the Sabbath day "they entered and found seats in the synagogue there", and the synagogue leaders invited Paul to preach.

At the beginning of Acts 14, we read that "the same thing happened in Iconium". Paul and Barnabas spoke in the synagogue, and a "huge number" of Jews and Greeks believed. Some Jews, however, rejected their teaching and "poisoned the minds of the Gentiles" against them. Nevertheless Paul and Barnabas stayed there "for quite some time" until plots against their lives forced them to flee the city.

In chapter 15 we are told that controversy broke out. Paul and Barnabas were appointed by the Antioch community to go to

Jerusalem to have the issue resolved. We should note that the controversy was over a Jewish issue:

> Some members from among the Pharisees stood up and proclaimed, "The Gentiles must be circumcised. They must be required to keep the Law of Moses." (15:5)

In chapter 17:

> They came to Thessalonika, where there was a Jewish synagogue. As was Paul's custom, he entered the synagogue and for three Sabbaths interacted with them on the basis of the scriptures...He declared, "This Jesus whom I proclaim to you is the Christ." (17:1-4)

Some Jews stirred up trouble, so they left town and went to Beroea:

> When they arrived, they went to the Jewish synagogue. The Beroean Jews were more honorable than those in Thessalonika. This was evident in the great eagerness with which they accepted the word and examined the scriptures each day to see whether Paul and Silas's teaching was true. Many came to believe, including a number of reputable Greek women and many Greek men. (17:10)

From Beroea, Paul travelled to Athens, and once again preached in the synagogue as well as in the market place:

He began to interact with the Jews and Gentile God-worshipers in the synagogue. He also addressed whoever happened to be in the marketplace each day. (17:17)

He then moved onto Corinth where:

Every Sabbath he interacted with people in the synagogue, trying to convince both Jews and Greeks. (18:4)

The pattern of contact through the Jewish community continued at Ephesus where again "he entered the synagogue and interacted with the Jews". (18:19) Later, he returned to Ephesus and preached in the synagogue for three months. However:

Some people closed their minds. They refused to believe and publicly slandered the Way. As a result, Paul left them, took the disciples with him, and continued his daily interactions in Tyrannus' lecture hall. This went on for two years... (19:8-10)

It is clear from these texts that Paul took his message about "the Way" outside the synagogues and into the market places where he encountered a Greek and Roman audience. While he did this as a Jew convinced of "the Way" of Jesus, he had to articulate his message in a manner that resonated with and responded to the questions and issues of Greek and Roman religious thought. This was not an easy task.

Judaism saw its role as establishing the reign of God on earth through systems of equality, compassion and justice for all. Its religious focus was on a personal God who interacted with the earthly world, a God who heard prayers and would respond to the cry of the poor. God was good; creation was good; and heaven and earth were both blessed with the Breath of God. The issue of life after death, immortality, had not been significant in Jewish thought until the revolt of the Maccabees against Greek rule in the second century before Jesus. It arose as an issue at that time from the belief that God could surely be trusted to reward those who died defending God's name and His chosen people. At the time of Jesus, though, the question of life after death was still a debatable issue in Judaism.

The Greeks and Romans, in stark contrast, had a strong interest in immortality. The Greeks considered earth to be inherently defective by its very nature as a changing, material reality. There could be no basic, lasting goodness here. There was no hope for immortality in this temporal world. That could only exist in the heavenly realm of the gods, of the One, of Pure Thought. The dominant religious question of the Greek-Roman world in which Paul found himself in the market places and elsewhere beyond the synagogues was: how can humans gain access to the heavenly realm and so attain immortality? Paul had to present Jesus as the answer to that question otherwise his preaching would fall on deaf ears, and Judaism would continue to be an oddity to the Greek-Roman intellectual and religious world.

The necessity to engage a religious worldview so different from that of Judaism and the necessity to present Jesus as the answer to the questions arising from that worldview led Paul to present Jesus in much the same way the Greeks and Romans presented their semi-gods. Jesus became the hero who had conquered the forces of evil and won access to the heavenly realm. Paul attributed to Jesus the same titles already bestowed on the Greek-Roman semi-gods and on the Roman Emperors, such as Savior, Son of God and Lord. Paul also used another title, one with a long history in Judaism, to bring his message about Jesus to Jews, pagans, Greeks and Romans. It was "christos", "the anointed one". Paul presented Jesus as "the Christ". As we saw earlier, he bestowed on "christos" a meaning, role and significance far beyond how Jesus would have applied the word to himself.

Paul's preaching about "the Christ" shifted the focus from Jesus revealing God here-with-us to Jesus as the unique pathway to the God who lived in heaven. Paul effectively fit Jesus into a worldview and into concerns Jesus had shown no interest in. Paul's preaching and writing led the early Jesus movement into concerns about the God who withheld forgiveness for sin and who had denied access to his heavenly home. In using a term familiar to Jews for responding to the Greeks, Paul surely hoped his teaching about "the Christos" would bridge the gap between two significantly different religious worldviews. Unfortunately, the effect was quite different. His Christology ultimately set the scene for the break from Judaism with the claims that only through faith in Jesus "the Christ" could anyone be sure of God's forgiveness and gain access to heaven. It also set up centuries of argument about who Jesus had to be in order to accomplish the task of bridging the chasm between heaven (God) and exiled humanity on earth.

While it is beyond the scope of this book to explore the development of Christology in the Christian Scriptures in any depth, it is imperative to identify how some of its key aspects changed the way Christians came to think about Jesus.

We find early expressions of the Christology in Peter's speech to the "Israelites" in the Acts of the Apostles:

> The Lord will provide a season of relief from the distress of this age and he will send Jesus whom he handpicked to be your Christ. Jesus must remain in heaven until the restoration of all things, about which God spoke long ago through his holy prophets. (3:20-22)

Let us keep in mind that the Acts of the Apostles was written well after Paul's time. The speech put on Peter's lips reflects Paul's earliest understanding of "Christos" in his first letter to the Thessalonians in which he wrote that Jesus had been taken into heaven where he became "the Christ" who would deliver humanity from God's "wrath" at the end times:

> You turned to God from idols. As a result, you are serving the living and true God, and you are waiting

for his Son from heaven. His Son is Jesus, who is the one he raised from the dead and who is the one who will rescue us from the coming wrath. (1:9-10)

The use of "Son" here does not identify Jesus with God. Jesus is still the human person raised into heaven by God.

In this letter to the Thessalonians, Paul described how he imagined Jesus would return as "the Christ" in Paul's own lifetime:

> The Lord himself will come down from heaven with the signal of a shout by the head angel and a blast on God's trumpet. First, those who are dead in Christ will rise. Then, we who are living and still around will be taken up together with them in the clouds to meet with the Lord in the air. That way we will always be with the Lord. (4:16-17)

Paul's thinking transformed the role of Jesus, "the human one" concerned with this world, into "the Christ", a heavenly figure associated with the end times and deliverance from "the coming wrath". This is not how Jesus understood his role. It is not what he preached.

When it became clear that the end times were not imminent, Paul had to adapt his thinking about the role of "the Christ". He did this by focusing on the resurrection. The resurrection of Jesus had always been pivotal, but Paul broadened its significance. He taught that making peace with God and the sending of God's Spirit upon a sinful world were dependent on it. He believed that no human being had access to heaven before God raised Jesus into heaven. He imagined that because of Adam's sin the world was estranged from God, and that there was no way humanity could be at peace with God or win God's forgiveness. He believed the resurrection of Jesus was God's seal of approval of Jesus and that now in heaven, as "the Christ", Jesus had "won" access to God, ensured God's forgiveness and sent God's Spirit down from heaven upon his followers.

These texts from Paul's Letter to the Romans illustrate his thinking:

> Since we have been made righteous through his faithfulness, combined with our faith, we have peace with God through our Lord Jesus Christ. (5:1)

> God shows his love for us, because while we were still sinners Christ died for us. So, now that we have been made righteous by his blood, we can be even more certain that we will be saved from God's wrath through him. (5:9)

> The wages that sin pays are death, but God's gift is eternal life in Christ Jesus our Lord. (6:23)

> God sent his own Son to deal with sin in the same body as humans who are controlled by sin. (8:3)

If anyone does not have the Spirit of Christ, they do
not belong to him. If Christ is in you, the Spirit is your
life." (8:9-10)

You received a Spirit that shows you are adopted as
God's children. (8:15)

That is why Christ died and lived: so that he might be
Lord of both the dead and the living. (14:9)

The time has come to challenge the basis of Paul's Christology,
to scrutinize his understanding of God, to contrast his thinking
with the teaching of Jesus, and to explore how today's cosmology might contribute to this critical task.

Paul's thinking and imagination are in stark contrast with Jesus'
belief and practice.

Jesus saw goodness in people and called upon them to recognize
God's Spirit present and active in their lives. He urged people to
trust in a God whose compassion and forgiveness were beyond
measure. He challenged people to convert from notions of a
punitive God. He told stories designed to lead people into a
trusting relationship with their God. He preached as someone
immersed in and convinced of a God whose graciousness was
bestowed freely on all people. Jesus understood people to be
intimately connected with God in their everyday loving.

Paul saw things very differently. Rather than seeing the goodness in people, Paul believed humans were controlled by sin. For

Paul, there was no possibility of definitive peace with God, not even through adherence to the Jewish Law. He taught that only "the Christ" could, and did, obtain that peace for us. Whereas Jesus preached a God of boundless forgiveness, Paul preached a God whose forgiveness was conditional. So Paul preached about "the Christ" being "sent" to die for "ungodly people" and that only through the "blood" of Jesus could humans be certain of being saved from "God's wrath".

We see more of Paul's thinking in 1 Corinthians:

> Christ died for our sins in line with the scriptures. (15:4)

> If Christ hasn't been raised, then your faith is worthless; you are still in your sins, and what's more, those who have died in Christ are gone forever. If we have a hope in Christ only in this life, then we deserve to be pitied more than anyone else. (15:16-19)

Paul consistently substitutes "Christ" for "Jesus". This is an extraordinary development. In changing Jesus into "the Christ" who supposedly won peace with and forgiveness from God, Paul effectively devalued Jesus and his preaching. Paul's Christology is totally at odds with how Jesus perceived his role. It is clear that Jesus never told people that God's forgiveness was conditional. It is clear he never told people that there was no hope of them being at peace with God unless he sacrificed his life for them. It is clear that he neither believed nor taught that God had disconnected from people.

Paul led Christian theology into literalizing the Adam and Eve story and into the belief that after Adam every person on this planet was born and died into a state of separation from God. With this theological foundation, it was inevitable that Christianity became a religion focused on "the Christ" who changed God's mind and attitude towards humanity.

In 1 Corinthians 8:6, Paul pushed his claims about "the Christ" even further:

> There is one God the Father. All things come from him and we belong to him. And there is one Lord Jesus Christ. All things exist through him and we live through him.

To attribute the existence of all things to the "Lord Jesus Christ" is strikingly gratuitous. It may be a grand idea, but it has no basis in reality. It is a monumental leap from anything Jesus taught. It is a construct of Paul's visionary imagination.

Paul's thinking was undoubtedly influenced by Jewish thought about the "Wisdom" of God. It would have helped Paul to have Jewish listeners or readers able to identify his "Christ" with the Wisdom of God. Wisdom was sometimes personified as God's companion, always there with God, but also coming down from heaven to visit earth, and, not being recognized, returning to heaven.

In the apocalyptic book of I Enoch, chapter 42:1-2, Wisdom

...found no place in which she could dwell,

but a dwelling place was found for her in the heavens.

Then Wisdom went forth to dwell with the children of the people, but she found no dwelling place.

So Wisdom returned to her own place, and she settled permanently among the angels.

In Philippians 2:6-11 we find the same pattern of pre-existence, descent from heaven, rejection, and ascent to heaven for "the Christ", followed by exaltation:

Though he was in the form of God,

he did not consider being equal to God something to exploit.

But he emptied himself by taking the form of a slave

and by becoming like human beings.

When he found himself in the form of a human,

he humbled himself by becoming obedient to the point of death, even death on a cross.

Therefore, God highly honored him and gave him a name above all names, so that at the name of Jesus everyone in heaven, on earth, and under the earth might bow and confess that Jesus Christ is Lord, to the glory of God the Father.

We need to understand that this connection of "the Christ" with Wisdom is imaginative. This is not an unchanging truth revealed by God through one of his chosen male writers. This is Paul, attempting as best he could to make his passionate understanding of "the Christ" acceptable to Jews as well as to the Greeks and Romans. It is visionary and it is grand, but that does not make it real. Even in his own lifetime, Paul's visionary ideas created tension. Followers of the Way soon found themselves in conflict with their Jewish religion.

While Jesus' preaching about establishing the kingdom of God on earth could readily resonate with Jewish belief and practice, Paul's teaching about "the Christ" offended many Jews. It seemed to undermine the importance of the Law and it made God's forgiveness and presence dependent on a human person. Paul was also clearly elevating Jesus to a status very close to that of God Himself.

It was inevitable that Judaism would take a stand against teachings deemed incompatible with its basic beliefs and practice.

6

....

THE BREAK WITH JUDAISM

Christians commonly believe that Pentecost is uniquely a Christian feast and that it marks the beginning of the Christian religion. Such is not the case. The Jewish religion had its own feast of Pentecost fifty days after Passover. It commemorated the giving of the Torah at Mount Sinai. It also celebrated the annual harvesting and the bringing of the first fruits to the Temple. Early Christian preaching and writing simply adapted the feast to fit the emerging Christology and proclaimed a new beginning, with the risen Jesus sending the Spirit of God down from heaven upon his followers.

Even with this adaptation, the followers of Jesus in the middle of the first century would not have understood Pentecost as the birth of a new religion. It was perceived as the birth of a "church", or more correctly, an "ecclesia".

In the New Testament the word "ecclesia" is used well over a hundred times to designate the people who gathered in the name of Jesus. The word is often translated as "church", and loses some of its essential meaning in the process. "Ecclesia" stems from the Greek words, *ek*, which means *out of*; and *klesis* which means *a calling*. In Athens, the ecclesia was the assembly of elected representatives who governed the city.

The use of "ecclesia" for their gatherings by the followers of Jesus would have been provocative. It signified a new way for society to organize itself, around the story of Jesus, the "Christ", the ruler of heaven and earth. People were being called out of, summoned from, the civil story of Caesar as king into allegiance to Jesus, the Christ.

The Acts of the Apostles mentions other "churches" or communities being formed in the name of Jesus, including those in Ephesus, Corinth and Rome. What these "churches" had in common was that they were essentially Jewish. They were founded by Jews to expand Judaism through preaching "the Way" of Jesus and proclaiming Jesus as "the Christ".

Chapter 19 of the Acts of the Apostles reveals an interesting facet of Paul's establishment of the ecclesia in Ephesus where he encountered opposition from fellow Jews. It seems that the opposition was not only about converts, but about Paul's version of "the Way" itself. Some Jews "spoke evil" about it. We saw in the previous chapter that Paul's preaching went well beyond anything Jesus had preached. It is not surprising that some Jews who listened to Paul began to object about where his thinking was taking them, especially when he undermined the primacy of the Law which was considered to be God's greatest gift to Judaism.

Paul, however, did not live to see the final split between the Jewish followers of Jesus, like himself, and the Jewish religion. The year of his death is uncertain, though most scholars place it in Rome, in the year 67. If that year is correct, Paul may have lived long enough to hear disturbing news from Jerusalem about the Jewish revolt against Roman rule in the year 66. The uprising eventually resulted in the destruction of Jerusalem and the Temple by the Roman army in 70.

It was at about this time that the first Gospel, Mark, appeared.

Mark's Gospel begins with the statement: *"The beginning of the gospel of Jesus the Christ, the Son of God."* Following this clear statement, the writer takes his readers or listeners back forty years or so and tells the story as if people in Jesus' lifetime did not clearly understand who Jesus was. The writer reveals to the reader or listener that the "Christos" moment occurred at the baptism of Jesus. This was a significant shift in the development of Christology.

Whereas Paul, in the years before Mark wrote, placed the "Christos" moment in heaven after the resurrection, Mark portrays the "Christos" moment at the baptism. This marks a completely new theological understanding and interpretation. The "Christos" moment was brought from heaven to earth, into Jesus' lifetime, and presented as if Jesus was aware of it. This is a monumental shift from Jesus' awareness of himself as some-one "anointed" or called by God to "preach the good news to the poor". In Mark's Gospel Jesus became "the Christ" figure of Paul's theology at his baptism. Jesus, the human one, would henceforth always be overshadowed in Christian understanding by the injection of Paul's "Christ" into his earthly life.

A decade or so later, the gospels of Luke and Matthew appeared. In these gospels the "Christos" moment comes even earlier in Jesus' life. Both gospels give Jesus a miraculous conception as a sign that he was indeed out of the ordinary, as befitting "the Christ". The writers of these two gospels were influenced by Greek and Roman religious stories about the births of their "savior" figures, and by Jewish "annunciation" stories. Both influences appear in the stories around Jesus' conception and birth.

These were new stories. Paul seems to have had no knowledge of them. It is important to understand that these stories about Jesus' birth emerged *after* Paul elevated Jesus to the status of "the Christ", the savior of the world, the heavenly Lord. They are stories that emerged from and are dependent on Paul's theology. Scripture scholars know and teach that the stories are not factual. They are "Christ" stories, not biographical stories about Jesus' actual birth. Any Roman Catholic doctrines about Mary or Jesus which rely on interpreting these stories as historical fact, for example, the virginal conception of Jesus, would not be supported by the Roman Catholic Church's own scriptural scholarship. That scholarship, however, rarely permeates the pews on Sundays because the doctrine and its origins cannot be questioned in any way. Many Roman Catholics still find it hard to believe, for example, that the Annunciation of an angel to Mary is not factual. The reason for their difficulty is simple: they have never been given any understanding of when and why the story originated.

Matthew's Gospel is particularly interesting in its presentation of "the Christ". The gospel was written within a Jewish community where the followers of Jesus still considered themselves faithful to Judaism. This was around fifty years after Jesus died and a decade or so after the destruction of Jerusalem and the Temple. The Pharisee leaders of the synagogues were trying desperately to sustain Jewish faith and practice in the face of such devastation. And right there in their communities were the followers of Jesus. The problem was not that these people followed Jesus, but that they were influenced by Paul's preaching about "the Christ". Paul's theology undermined the authority of the synagogue leaders because it proclaimed "Jesus the Christ", not the Law, as the basis of relationship with God. Paul's theology seemed to downplay the importance of the Law. That would have been viewed as an attack on the heart and soul of Judaism. The followers of Jesus consequently found themselves on the wrong side of their own religious leadership, even to the point of being excluded from community life.

Matthew 10:16-42 offers an insight to what happened. The verses appear to be warnings from Jesus about a time of persecution that will come upon his followers. However, it is more likely that the writer, experiencing persecution and discord within his own Jewish community because of Jesus, put words on Jesus' lips as a way of exhorting the Jewish followers of Jesus to hold fast in tough times:

> They will hand you over to councils and they will beat you in their synagogues...Everyone will hate you on account of my name... (10: 17, 22)

In this climate of tension and division, the writer of Matthew's Gospel attempted to present Jesus as a religious leader faithful to Judaism. It is a counterbalance to Paul's thinking about the heavenly "Christ". The Gospel presents Jesus as a faithful Jew concerned with keeping the spirit of the Law and establishing the "kingdom of God" here on earth. Its presentation of Jesus resonates with the promise made by Moses, "The Lord God will raise up for you a prophet from your brethren as he raised me up. You shall listen to him in whatever he tells you." (Deuteronomy 18:15, 18). The author of Matthew's Gospel goes a step further than asserting that Jesus is this anointed prophet. He presents Jesus to the Jewish community as a revered figure like Moses. The birth narratives are constructed in such a way that the readers link Jesus with Moses. For example, there is a slaughter of infants, and refuge in Egypt. Imitating Moses, Jesus goes up a mountain to present the Beatitudes whereas in Luke's gospel the event takes place on "a level place" (6:17). Even Joseph's father's name is changed, from "Heli" in Luke's

Gospel (3:23), to "Jacob" in Matthew's Gospel to fit with the well-known story of Jacob and his son Joseph in Egypt.

Chapters 5 to 7 are the highlight of Matthew's gospel. In essence they present "the Way" of Jesus. Far from any thinking that Jesus' preaching undermined the centrality of the Law and its importance, the gospel presents Jesus challenging Jews to live the spirit of the Law. Any great Jewish teacher could summarize the Law as: *Love God and neighbor graciously and wholeheartedly*. This is the message of God's anointed one, as promised by Moses. In Matthew's Gospel, Jesus, like Moses, was anointed, called, chosen by God to be a great Jewish leader. The writer wants his readers and hearers to understand that followers of Jesus are not being unfaithful to Judaism. Rather they gather around Jesus, a faithful Jew, who proclaimed his intention to fulfill the Law, not displace it:

> Take note, for I say to you, until heaven and earth pass away not an iota, not a dot, will pass from the law until all is accomplished. Whoever, therefore, relaxes even one of the least of these commandments and teaches others to do so shall be called least in the kingdom of heaven; but whoever does them and teaches them shall be called great in the kingdom of heaven. (5:17-20)

It is possible the writer thought Paul belonged among "the least in the kingdom of God" for his teaching about the limitations of the Law. The passage may have been intended as a corrective to Paul's influence.

Matthew's Gospel reflects a final effort by Jewish followers of Jesus within a Jewish community to have their faithfulness to Judaism recognized by leadership in the community. "Look!" they proclaimed, "We are faithful to Moses and the Law! Look at what Jesus preached about the "kingdom of God" and how we are to live. Jesus is the anointed one promised by Moses himself! Why are you persecuting us?"

They lost the argument. They could not overcome the suspicion Jewish religious leaders had about the supremacy of Paul's "Christ". It was only a matter of time before Judaism distanced itself from Paul's Christology. The followers of Jesus then found themselves unwillingly ostracized from their parent religion.

This led to the eventual separation of the followers of Jesus from their Jewish communities. It was this separation, not Pentecost Sunday, that marked the birth of a new religion.

Paul did not start this religion. Most likely he would never have envisaged a new religion. But his teaching about "the Christ" was ultimately responsible for the split. Once the split came, the new religious movement began to articulate its identity and role in line with Paul's Christology which had caused the split, rather than focus on the teaching of Jesus, which, as Matthew's Gospel tried to show, was compatible with Judaism.

The new religion adopted the word that had been used to describe those who embraced Paul's theology, "Christian". It taught that its "Christ" had opened the gates of heaven, had won God's forgiveness, had sent God's Spirit down upon earth, and was co-creator with God. It maintained that this religion was founded by Christ himself to bring heavenly salvation to the world. It proclaimed that only through faith in Jesus, "the Christ", could people get into heaven. This belief readily evolved into the assertion that membership of this new group was essential to attain eternal life with God.

"Come," said this new religion, "come into our fold and we will guarantee you a place in heaven."

John's Gospel appeared toward the end of the first century. In the centuries that followed, the author of this gospel was often referred to as the "Theologian". That in itself should alert us to the fact that this gospel is a theological interpretation of Jesus. In John's Gospel, "the Christ" now became the pre-existing "Word of God" who dwelt in the heavens and came down to earth as the "true light". To "all who received him, who believed in his name, he gave power to become children of God." (1:12). We see here another significant shift away from the preaching of Jesus. Jesus had recognized and affirmed God's presence with people and had called on them to act upon it and establish the kingdom of God on earth. He had affirmed people as "children of God" when they mourned, when they forgave, when they were peace-makers, when they were pure of heart. John's Gospel, in line with Paul's theology, asserts that only through belief in Jesus as the heavenly "Christ" figure could people receive "power to become children of God."

More than the other gospels, the gospel of John extolled "the Christ" Jesus as pivotal for access to God. It is not surprising that it became the favorite gospel of the Church. Church leaders through the centuries, including, not surprisingly, the present Pope, have interpreted the statement that, "No one can come to the Father except through me" (14:6), to mean that faith in Jesus, through membership of the Church, is indispensable for access to God. Recall what we saw earlier from the Vatican's Declaration, *Dominus Iesus:*

> Above all else it must be firmly believed that the Church, a pilgrim on earth, is necessary for salvation; the one Christ is the mediator and the way of salvation." (#.20)

> God has willed that the Church founded by Jesus Christ be the instrument for the salvation of humanity. (#.21)

Scholars know that the speeches put on Jesus' lips throughout John's gospel are not the words of Jesus. The words are a long way removed from the reality of Jesus, "the son of man" who preached the urgent need to establish God's reign on earth. The speeches call attention to Jesus, not to the kingdom of God. "I am this ... I am that ... Before Abraham I ...I go to prepare a place for you... Unless I go the Spirit will not come ..." These are not the words of Jesus who walked the roads of Galilee. They are speeches composed in the light of Paul's Christology and designed to give the new religion strong institutional identity apart from Judaism. They were composed in a worldview that understood God really lived elsewhere, that this God had "sent" the pre-existent Christ down from the heavenly realm, and that the Christ had to go back up to the heavenly realms in order to "send" God's Spirit down upon the followers of Jesus, and only on them!

Thereafter, institutional Christian leadership locked itself into this theological worldview. This theology was then cemented into creeds and doctrines that supposedly can never change.

The reality is that this theology and Paul's vision of "the Christ" on which it depends cannot withstand any realistic scrutiny in the twenty-first century. A God who lives in heaven? A God who locked people out? A world devoid of God's presence? A God who would not forgive? A God who gets angry? God's Spirit waiting in heaven for something to happen on earth before "coming down"? A God who allows access to "Himself" only if people join a particular religion?

And, if such questions are not enough to raise concerns today about Paul's theology, we can also add that his theology is an outright contradiction of Jesus' belief that the Divine Presence was always present to and active in people here on earth.

Roman Catholic leadership knows no other way to articulate the role of the Church in the world today except through this unreal theological interpretation of Jesus. The present Pope, along with most of the bishops he has gathered around him as "defenders of the faith", believes that the future of the Church depends on protecting this theology. This inflexibility allows no possibility of discussion and no possibility of presenting Jesus to the modern world apart from its outdated Christology. That is why theologians are silenced and women religious threatened with dire consequences if they raise questions Rome thinks could disturb this theology. This is why the CDF adopts the intellectually dishonest practice of demanding unqualified assent to doctrines. Catholics are obliged to assent to doctrines shaped in a pre-scientific worldview and used by Church leadership to protect its unique identity and authority in the world. Doctrine is absolute truth. Doctrine cannot be questioned. Doctrine has been sanctioned by God Himself. Doctrine is about God's Church. The CDF exists to protect this doctrine and "God's Church" from any questions arising from factual data or scholarly research.

It is time to question doctrine and its place in the Church and the protection given it by men who use it as a control mechanism to ensure they are answerable to no one.

It is time to recognize and name what doctrine really is. It is "institutional theology". It is theology geared to give the institution special status, identity and power.

7

....

IT'S TIME

The most significant question that has engaged the minds of Christian theologians throughout the centuries has been: *Who was Jesus if he, and only he, gained access to the heavens where God lives?*

The answer to that question has been and still is used to determine whether someone is a "true Christian" or a heretic, dishonorable and unworthy to be a member of the Church.

It is time to consider this important question dispassionately and to bring honest thinking to the table. This is not easy to do because the "correct" answer to the question leads to the conclusion that Jesus is the incarnation of a God who lives in heaven. Only if Jesus is "consubstantial" with God, could he win access to God's dwelling place. Surely you are not going to deny the Incarnation! Surely you are not going to deny that Jesus is God incarnate! Surely you are not going to deny the doctrine that has become the bedrock of Christianity!

The problem is that people start with the conclusion: Jesus is the unique incarnation of a heavenly God. They are fearful of any thinking that might disturb that conclusion. They have been taught that the conclusion is absolute, certain truth beyond any questioning. They fear that Christianity would collapse as a religion if that conclusion were openly questioned. This fear needs to be addressed.

Christianity would not collapse. Rather, it would return, as it should, to focus on Jesus and his concern to make the Divine Presence visible in our human interactions. It would tell the story of Jesus, not through the lens of Paul's worldview, but through the lens of contemporary understanding of the Divine Presence at work throughout the universe and in the human species. It would have a wonderful and challenging story to bring to our world.

Furthermore, if the conclusion that Jesus is the unique incarnation of a heavenly God arises from faulty premises and an outmoded religious worldview, then there is no intellectual integrity or honesty in Church leadership or the CDF when they assert that the conclusion is an act of faith and no questioning is permitted.

The first thing that needs to be established about the question, *Who was Jesus if he, and only he, gained access to the heavens where God lives?* is that getting people into heaven was not the concern of Jesus. Yes, there are elements of the Pauline "Christ" written into the Gospel accounts, especially in John's Gospel.

However, when we look closely at Jesus' preaching to the crowd about the kingdom of God and how people must act in order to bring about this "kingdom", we see Jesus affirming the Divine Presence in people and challenging them to give expression to it. If Jesus did not see disconnection from a heavenly God as an issue he had to address, why did it become an issue for his followers?

The next important point is to consider about the question is whether this is our question today.

Christians who want their faith to resonate with their twenty-first century understanding of earth's place in the universe and a notion of "God" that is expansive enough to embrace what we mean by "everywhere" today, have moved beyond the religious and Greek worldview of two thousand years ago. They have moved on from scriptural literalism and the story of a "fall" when the human species emerged. They do not believe that the Divine Presence was absent from indigenous religions. They believe that anyone, at any time, in any place, who lived in love "lived in God and God lived in them". Their religious worldview is not one of a primordial disconnection from and later reconnection with a heavenly "God", but one that embraces the reality of the Divine Presence always, everywhere active.

In other words, they do not believe in a "God" who locked people out. They see that Jesus himself never believed in such an understanding of God. For them this historically significant question is considered to be irrelevant. It is not the question raised today by either their worldview or by their fidelity to the teaching of Jesus. The question belongs to Paul's worldview, to his concept of "the Christ", and to a Church that embraced Paul's Christology in order to establish the Church's unique identity in the world.

It is time to rescue Jesus from this distracting issue about getting people into heaven.

It is time to rescue Jesus from the Pauline "Christ" theology, the doctrines, the prayer forms and the institutional claims to absolute power and authority that go with it. It is time to stop using "Christ" as Jesus' name. "Christ" does not elevate Jesus. It distorts his role, distracts from the urgency of his message, and most unfortunately, inflicts on Christians the mistaken belief that Jesus was really not like the rest of us in his humanity.

There is nothing new with the realization that Paul's thinking radically changed how Christianity presented itself to the world and came to articulate its unique role in the world. There is nothing new about discussion on the human Jesus in contrast with the divine Christ. There is nothing new about a quest to unearth the "real Jesus" below the layers of Pauline Christology. There is nothing new about debating the merits of a "low Christology" which focuses on the human reality of Jesus and builds from there, opposed to a "high Christology" which emphasizes the divine Christ and Jesus' awareness of his "divine nature". That debate is almost as old as Christianity.

What is new is that for the first time in Christian history, we have an emerging "new story" about our universe, about the activity of the Divine Presence, about ourselves, about the inter-connection of all things, that is not biblically based. It is a story that encompasses everyone and everything.

This story demands a new way to understand Jesus.

The task of the Church in any age is to bring the freeing and challenging teaching of Jesus to the world and to the age in which it finds itself. The new story presents the most monumental agenda ever to confront the Christian religion. The Council of Nicaea, the Reformation and Vatican II almost pale into insignificance in comparison. Christianity has to make the most radical change imaginable. It has to return its focus to the human reality of Jesus. It has to focus on Jesus' preaching about this world. It has to honor the reality of the Divine Presence everywhere, in all people. It has to re-articulate its identity and its role in the world based on Jesus, not on Paul and not on gospels influenced by Paul's Christology.

The new story in which we want to understand Jesus brings a stark choice to Christianity: choose this story and articulate your religious beliefs in accord with it or remain in Paul's story which makes no sense to people educated in the new story.

This is new, indeed! This is not a debate about the merits of a low Christology against the merits of a high Christology. This is not a debate whether we should start with the human Jesus or start with Jesus the incarnate Son of God who came down from heaven. No, this is a choice which says that one of the alternatives has no basis in reality. You either make sense of Jesus in the light of what we know today *or* you choose to stay locked in a religious imagination and worldview that are irrelevant in the modern world. It is as simple as that.

Many Christians have made their choice and have walked away from formal participation in a religion that does not respect their intelligence and education. Their numbers are likely to keep increasing as long as institutional leadership is unwilling or unable to comprehend the seriousness of the situation. These Christians have not given up on Jesus and his importance to the world. The "Spirit of the Lord" is upon them as they try to articulate and live a Christian spirituality appropriate for these times.

As we have seen, we can readily place Jesus' message and his concern for the world in the context of the "new story" about the universe. What is more problematic is the task of rescuing him and the Christian religion from the Christology that developed after he died.

Paul never quoted Jesus for any of his theological beliefs. His authority for what he preached about "the Christ" did not come from anything Jesus said or did in his lifetime.

The gospels followed Paul. The authors wrote back into the story of Jesus a Christology that Jesus knew nothing about and made it appear he was well aware of it.

Christian doctrine followed suit. Doctrine built on Paul and the Gospels. However, doctrine then went much further and read back into the story of Jesus a "divine nature", complete with divine knowledge and divine will. Doctrine made Jesus into someone he would not, as a faithful Jew, have considered himself to be.

According to Christian doctrine as expounded by Joseph Ratzinger, the CDF and *The Catechism of the Catholic Church* Jesus knew he was God incarnate, knew the will of the Father, and knew he had to die in order to win God's forgiveness for sinful humanity. Doctrine insists that the divine will was always in charge over Jesus' human will emotions, as these two paragraphs from the Catechism indicate:

> By its union to the divine wisdom in the person of the Word incarnate, Christ enjoyed in his human knowledge the fullness of understanding of the eternal plans he had come to reveal. What he admitted to not knowing in this area, he elsewhere declared himself not sent to reveal.(#474)

> Similarly, at the sixth ecumenical council, Constantinople III in 681, the Church confessed that Christ possesses two wills and two natural operations, divine and human. They are not opposed to each other, but cooperate in such a way that the Word made flesh willed humanly in obedience to

his Father all that he had decided divinely with the
Father and the Holy Spirit for our salvation. Christ's
human will "does not resist or oppose but rather
submits to his divine and almighty will." *(475)*

Christianity has always insisted that Jesus was "really and truly
human" like the rest of us. However, as the above quotes indicate, the Church wants Christians to believe that Jesus did not
experience uncertainty or live by faith as we do.

Is this the Jesus who walked the streets and byways of
Galilee?

It is time to question the institutional assertion that the only legitimate or acceptable way to think about Jesus is through Paul's
understanding and the worldview in which his understanding
was shaped. It is time to question the belief that because Paul's
writings are part of Scripture they cannot be questioned. It is
time to reflect on Jesus' life and ministry in a way that honors
his true humanity and avoids one man's mystical interpretation
of him.

It is time to reflect on Jesus with our twenty first century appreciation that he was the human expression of the Divine at work
in the universe.

It is time to see how this shift in the way we focus on Jesus
enhances our understanding and appreciation of Jesus as revealer

of the Divine Presence always and everywhere graciously present and active.

It is time to see how such reflection helps us to know Jesus better as friend, as companion, and as the "heart" of a genuine Christian spirituality.

It is time for us to push aside the theological "Christ" construct and reflect on some key incidents in Jesus' life.

....

8

THE BAPTISM OF JESUS. CHOICE

The writers of the Synoptic Gospels each brought Paul's Christology to their accounts of Jesus' life and ministry. The first Gospel, Mark, brought Paul's heavenly appointed "Christ" back into the life of Jesus. At his baptism "the heavens opened, the Spirit descended upon Jesus like a like a dove, and a voice came from heaven, 'Thou art my beloved son with whom I am well pleased.'" (1:11) Mark presented the baptism as the moment of revelation that Jesus was "the Christ".

Many Christians hear and read this as a factual account of what happened at the start of Jesus' public ministry. A more accurate way of approaching this story is to recognize it as a theological under-standing constructed *after* Jesus died and written back into his life. Mark took an important moment of choice in Jesus' life and overlaid it with a later theological perspective based on Pauline Christology. As with all "the Christ" overlays written back into gospel stories, this overshadows and minimizes the human experience of Jesus.

It is time to put aside the theological aspect of the baptism story and ask, "What was the human experience here?"

There came a moment in his life when Jesus committed himself to being a prophetical voice, to following the promptings of the Divine Presence within him, and to accepting the consequences. Now, that is a momentous decision for any human person to make. Jesus, like any of us making a major decision in life, surely prayed and spent considerable time reflecting on the pros and cons of his choice.

The human experience was of a man immersed in the ideals of his religious tradition who anguished about the state of the world that must have seemed godless to him.

The human experience was that this man had a dream for peace and a better world, a dream that is written deep into all of us as the prompting of the Divine within the human.

The human experience was that this man felt a movement deep within him and he named it as the "Spirit of the Lord" upon him.

The human experience was that this man recognized this same Spirit in the people around him and yearned for them to be aware of it as clearly as he was aware of the Spirit within himself.

The human experience was that this man set himself to address whatever prevented people from giving expression to the Spirit he knew was in them.

The human experience was that this man had to determine how to go about the role he believed he was called to fulfill.

The human experience was that this man faced a daunting task if he was to convert people to his vision, and he knew it.

The theological overlay, however, especially when it is linked with the Vatican's insistence that the Divine will was always in control of Jesus' humanity, takes away from Jesus any search, any struggle, any doubts, and any real temptations for him to walk away from such an onerous choice. It paints a picture of Jesus so sure of his identity and his role that he is nothing like the rest of us in our search for identity and integrity. This Jesus would not have to live the beatitudes the way we strive to live them. No, the divine nature and the divine will would make everything absolutely clear and certain to him. There would be no struggle whatever with decisions to be made. The divine will and knowledge would rule his daily life. He would not know what it is to struggle to be pure in heart, to be merciful, to be faithful to the promptings of the Spirit, or to be a peacemaker. Prayer would never have to involve reflection, discernment and choice.

This Jesus cannot genuinely offer this invitation to a relationship of friendship:

> Come to me, all you who are struggling hard and carrying heavy loads, and I will give you rest. Put on my yoke, and learn from me. I am gentle and humble in

heart. And you will find rest for yourselves. My yoke
is easy and my burden is light. (Matthew 11:28-30)

The way Christians traditionally understand the baptism of Jesus
is a perfect example of how Paul's Christology removed Jesus
from the realm of ordinary human experience and turned him
into someone fundamentally unlike the rest of us. The approach
has been, and still is, "See, he knew he was the Christ, the Son
of God, who came to save the world from sin. See, God spoke
to him directly from heaven." Christians generally have no
idea that this heavenly announcement proclaims a belief about
Jesus that in reality he knew nothing about. Consequently, they
believe that Jesus always knew he was "the Christ" who knew
he had to die for sinful humanity and win God's forgiveness and
friendship.

With this as their understanding of Jesus' baptism, it is not surprising that most Christians find it hard to believe that Jesus was
really human like them and knew what it was like to struggle
with choices and commitment.

It is only when we suspend assent to the theological construct of
"the Christ" that we can relate with the human Jesus who really
knew the pain and difficulties of human existence. Only then can
empathy and friendship with him develop.

It is time to question any theological thinking that effectively
strips Jesus of normal human experience.

It is time to ask what right has Paul's or anyone else's "Christology" to take away Jesus' capacity to relate with us in friendship and compassion.

It is time to ask why Christianity, especially Roman Catholicism, prefers correct theological thinking *about Jesus "the Christ"* over personal relationship *with Jesus, the human one.*

It is time to change the focus, time to see beyond or beneath the Christological overlays that permeate the Gospel accounts of Jesus' life and ministry, and come face to face, heart to heart, with Jesus, human like us, in his search for meaning and in his decision to stand up for what he believed.

....

9

JESUS AND POWERLESSNESS

My first book, *God is Near. Understanding a Changing Church*, was published in Australia in 1992. It had an Imprimatur and a Nihil Obstat from the Archdiocese of Melbourne and was launched by a bishop. In a chapter on prayer I invited readers to respond to the invitation of Jesus: *come, and learn of my heart; come, and establish a relationship of friendship with me.* I suggested that one of the best ways to do this was to take gospel stories and to imagine being with Jesus as a friend and to ask him what was he feeling or thinking about in any particular incident. In this way, hearts could touch in understanding, and genuine friendship with Jesus could develop. This type of prayer interaction could help people to move beyond knowing *about* Jesus to a sense of *knowing* him.

As part of this heart-speaking-to-heart process, I suggested that readers might ask Jesus questions that pertain to everyday human experience, such as, "Did you ever feel so weary that you felt like not continuing?" Or, "Did you ever want to marry?"

One of the gospel incidents I suggested for contemplation was from Matthew chapter 14, where Jesus hears the news of the brutal death of his cousin, John. I had used this particular gospel incident many times in retreats and workshops, inviting people to consider what Jesus may have felt on hearing the news. People had appreciated the exercise because the sharing of Jesus' reactions brought them closer to a Jesus who could understand their own pains. In *God Is Near*, I listed some of the sharing I heard from participants over the years.

The book was well received by Catholics in Australia and was reprinted seven times within five years.

On 15th July, 1997, the Superior General of the Missionaries of the Sacred Heart in Rome received a letter from the Congregatio Pro Doctrina Fidei (the CDF) stating:

> This Congregation has received many complaints over the years concerning doctrinal errors in a book authored by Fr Michael Morwood MSC.

> A study of the book has revealed that it indeed does contain doctrinal errors, especially with regard to the nature of Christ.

As is the practice with the CDF, the report that accompanied the letter was unsigned. There was no information about the actual number of complaints, about who made them or what qualifications these people held.

The report stated:

> Some points of the book present grave doctrinal problems. These primarily concern Jesus before the Resurrection. According to the author, Jesus, to be truly human, had to live by faith, not knowing with certainty that he was God, otherwise he would not have had either uncertainty, nor questioning, nor doubts, nor obscurity: *"If he knows, with certain knowledge, as a child that he is God, and if he knows everything God knows, then he does not have to live by faith; there is no uncertainty, no questioning, no searching, no act of faith required in times of doubt and darkness. However, for Jesus to be really human, he must live by faith. That is an essential part of being human"* (p. 17; cf. pp. 18-19). The faith of Jesus has been subjected to obscurity and even, in the passion, to temptations of desperation: *"Here was a man holding on to his beliefs about God in the midst of darkness and the temptation to despair."* (p. 23).

Regarding the passions of the soul, the author attributes some to Jesus which imply faithlessness and powerlessness; thus, for example, in learning of the news of the death of John the Baptizer: *"What is he feeling? It could be any number of deep feelings: shock, anger, regret, fear, powerlessness, loneliness, helplessness, abandonment, rage, concern, grief."* (p. 60). The reader is invited to formulate questions for Jesus: *"Did you ever long to be held by a woman? Did you want to marry?"* (p. 18).

The next line of the report delivered the CDF's judgment:

One cannot see how all these approaches and assertions can be compatible with the teachings of the Magisterium, right from the times of the Christological heresies. St. Leo the Great, although being a great defender of the integrity of the human nature of Jesus Christ against the errors of Eutiches, wrote: "He had no opposition in His flesh, nor did any lack of harmony in desires cause a conflict of wills. His bodily senses were vigorous without the law of sin; His emotions, which were real, were not tempted by allurements and did not give way to harmful influences since they were under the control of His divinity and His mind."

The Third Council of Constantinople excludes every resistance or reluctance of the human will of Jesus Christ in respect to the divine will (cf. DS 556).

The report goes on to say that:

> The recent opinion of some about the limited knowl-
> edge of the soul of Christ cannot be taught safely and
> must not be more favored than the ancient opinion
> about Jesus' universal knowledge.

As an aside, on the same day in 499 when he wrote the passage quoted above by the CDF, St Leo the Great wrote another
letter stating that Jesus "*was born in a 'new type of birth' in
that undefiled virginity experienced no concupiscence.*" Leo the
Great was hardly an authority on "bodily senses", emotions and
human nature.

With regard to the divine will controlling Jesus' decisions,
actions and emotional states, Leo was doing no more than thinking and teaching within the doctrine expounded by the Christian
Church to explain how Jesus could be both God and man in
order to gain access into heaven.

This doctrine about the divine will, elevated to absolute, "most
certain of all knowledge" status, leads the CDF to insist that
for Jesus to experience "*shock, anger, regret, fear, powerlessness, loneliness, helplessness, abandonment, rage, concern,
grief*" "implies faithlessness". The CDF condemns the idea that
Jesus actually experienced these emotions and struggled with
them or with any experience of powerlessness on the grounds
that this thinking is not "compatible with the teachings of the
Magisterium".

We need to ask: where did this doctrine about the divine will always being in control of everything Jesus did come from? What gave rise to it? Would we have it if Christianity had kept its focus on the teaching of Jesus rather than being distracted by Paul's grand vision of "the Christ" who won access to heaven? The doctrine serves no purpose for understanding the human Jesus as revealer of the Divine Presence among us. It only serves to keep off limits any questions about the worldview we inherited from Paul, a worldview that suits institutional Christianity's claim to uniqueness.

The great pity is, that for centuries, this and other doctrines about Jesus based on Paul's Christology have undermined the possibility of Christians responding heart to heart to Jesus' very personal, very human invitation to friendship. Instead, they have led to the conclusion that Jesus would not know our human struggles and that he never knew the anguish of holding on to faith in God's presence during tough times.

Let us return to Matthew's gospel chapter 14 which is a typical mixture of "the Christ" doing marvellous deeds, including feeding five thousand people and walking on water, and glimpses of the human Jesus. We want to focus on the human reality.

After hearing of John's death and then ministering to the crowd, Jesus sent his apostles away and "he went up onto a mountain by himself to pray. Evening came and he was alone." (14:23)

It is surely a worthwhile exercise for any friend of Jesus to wonder, and to ask him, what he might have prayed about that night. Did he need to process his grief, his anger, his loneliness or any regrets he had? Was he concerned that he might be next? Did he need to withdraw and find the inner strength from the Spirit within him to face an uncertain future? Did he consider giving up his preaching to the crowd, knowing his dream was not likely to come to fruition? Did he need to reflect on and pray about what to do next? Should he go to Jerusalem, or withdraw into safety?

This is a faithful and legitimate way of contemplating Jesus' reaction to the news of his cousin's death and his need for solitude and prayer. It is a way to be with him as friend and companion, as we would want him to be friend and companion with us in times of stress and upheaval. It is a way to appreciate the turning point in his life when in all probability he knew his life's dream was not going to be realized. He knew he would likely die without seeing what he wanted to see. He considered the options, and determined he would go to Jerusalem and stand up for what he believed. He was clear about what he was ready to die for. It was not for our sins. It was for what he believed and taught about God and the Kingdom here on earth.

This is the Jesus who resonates heart to heart with us as we realize we may never see "the Church" we want to see. This is the Jesus we need to know as we articulate what we really believe.

.₃ the Jesus we want to know whenever we find ourselves having to stand up and be counted for what we believe. This is the Jesus we as "Church" should be gathering around.

But, no, says the CDF. That would not be in accord with the teaching of the Magisterium. You cannot imply that Jesus' divine will and knowledge were not in control. That would reduce Jesus to being merely human. If he were merely human like us he would not be able to win God's forgiveness for sin and get us into heaven.

Two issues deserve our attention here. The first is the CDF's insistence that the primary goal of Jesus' ministry was gaining access to heaven, when clearly it was not. The second is the CDF's poor opinion of being human. Honoring Jesus as a wonderful expression of the Divine in human form does not denigrate Jesus. Rather, it enhances our appreciation of what it is to be human. His humanity reveals to us the same Divine Presence in our humanity. When we distort peoples' idea of Jesus with fanciful doctrine about a divine will over-riding his humanity, we do both Jesus and ourselves a disservice. It is a disservice to Jesus because it removes him from the human experience of living by faith in the midst of struggle. It is a disservice to ourselves because it prevents us from seeing and appreciating that Jesus lived our human condition and reveals to us that what was true of him is true of us - that we all give expression to the Divine Presence.

10

....

HOLY THURSDAY. COMMITMENT

We are accustomed to understand the events of Holy Thursday through the lens of doctrinal formulations about Jesus as "the Christ" who had a divine nature, a divine will and divine knowledge. We were taught to believe that at the Last Supper Jesus set up a new religion with its own cultic priesthood, that he instituted the Eucharist and that he bestowed on his male apostles the power to bring his Presence to the consecrated bread.

The reality is that none of this would have been known to the Jewish followers of Jesus in the twenty or so years after his death and before Paul. They knew Jesus died a Jew. They knew his teaching was concerned with "the Way", a radical way of living here on earth. They did not see themselves as members of a new religion apart from Judaism. We have seen that this way of viewing Jesus continued up to the time of the writing of Matthew's Gospel. Yes, they celebrated "eucharist", but they celebrated it as Jews, and brought their Jewish understanding to the celebration. Yes, the apostles were leaders in a new movement, but not one of them ever renounced their Judaism.

So, here is another choice to be made.

Do we choose to believe that at the Last Supper, "the Christ" with the divine will and divine knowledge set up a new religion? Do we make the only acceptable understanding of what happened at the meal an understanding that the Jewish people present, including Jesus, would never have entertained? Or do we choose to get beneath the theological overlay of "the Christ" at work the night before he died and encounter Jesus, the Jew, whose dream was shattered and who desperately wanted his Jewish companions to keep his dream alive?

The CDF insists there is no legitimacy to the alternative choice. The only possible choice is the one that supports institutional claims that God Himself founded this Church. It is the choice on which the notion of Apostolic Succession and the power and authority that go with it are founded. It is the choice that supports the claim that God wants everyone to belong to this Church. It is the choice that allows the CDF to maintain that Jesus actually ordained men into a new cultic priesthood separate from Judaism the night before he died. It is the choice that ensures that no Catholic theologian can publicly question what the Catholic Church officially teaches about Jesus founding the Catholic Church. It is a choice that dishonestly avoids the reality that the first "pope" was a married Jew who would not have considered himself the leader of a religion separate from Judaism.

Let us put aside the theological construct of "the Christ" setting up a new religion. Let us explore the human reality.

The human reality is that Jesus, the Jew, had a Passover meal with his Jewish friends. Let us, in a movement of friendship with Jesus, try to understand what might have been moving in his mind and heart as he came to the end of his life, knowing his ministry had failed. Let us take on board the image of a man who, when he came to Jerusalem for the last time, broke down and cried over what might have been. Let us imagine Jesus considering the small group of men and women gathered around him and thinking that the future of his dream and everything he was ready to die for rested with them. Only when we meet Jesus heart-to-heart in this way will we really understand and appreciate the true story of "eucharist".

Jesus took bread, broke it, and identified the gesture with himself. The point of the gesture was not to raise questions about how the bread *was* Jesus or *became* Jesus. Rather, it was Jesus' powerful way of expressing symbolically, *This is what it is like to be me.* What Jesus wanted his friends to see in the gesture was his willingness to give his all for what he believed, someone blessed and broken and given. Jesus wanted his friends to remember him this way. But, more than that, he asked them to eat the bread. The point of eating the bread was not to raise questions about what they were actually eating. That question would not have risen in the minds of Jews sharing a Passover meal that was permeated with the power of symbol. No, the obvious question here is: *To what were those present committing themselves if they took the bread from Jesus and ate it?* They would have realized that Jesus was symbolically asking for their commitment to carry on his dream and his ministry. He was asking if they, too, were willing to be blessed, broken and given.

It is in Jesus' human experience of pain, loss, dreaming, longing, friendship and commitment that we can find what Eucharist is really about. It is not about receiving something. Eucharist, in so far as it is connected with Jesus' actions the night before he died, was not intended to be about priests with special powers to bring a Presence that was not already with people. It was not to be about who can do this and who cannot. It was not to be about how it works. And it was most definitely not to be about making people dependent on a clerical middle-management for the celebration of "eucharist". It was, is, and always should be about serious commitment to the dream of Jesus.

It is obvious whose interests are served through focusing on doctrine about "the Christ" who set up a new religion and established Eucharist dependent on transubstantiation and priestly powers. This doctrine protects male institutional leadership in the Roman Catholic Church and its interests. It is the control mechanism they use to protect their status as chosen agents of God looking after God's Church. Consider the current theological and liturgical trend in the Roman Catholic Church. It is a return to the "unworthy" theology of former times, to heightened clericalism, to adoration, to bowing, and to making clear in peoples' minds they are dependent on the priest for Eucharist.

Consider also the developments in the past forty years on the question of women's ordination in the Roman Catholic Church. In 1994 in *Ordinatio Sacerdotalis,* Pope John Paul II declared that the Church had "no authority" to ordain women and that this judgement was a "definitive" decision to be held by all Catholics. A year later, the CDF went further and attempted to raise the decision to the status of an infallible decision:

This teaching requires definitive assent, since, founded on the written Word of God, and from the beginning constantly preserved and applied in the Tradition of the Church, it has been set forth infallibly by the ordinary and universal Magisterium.

In an accompanying letter, Cardinal Joseph Ratzinger, then head of the CDF, called on bishops around the world to ensure that "theologians, pastors of souls and religious" do not propose any contrary or ambiguous positions on this issue.

Cardinal Ratzinger should have included the Pontifical Biblical Commission in his list of groups who are not to question the CDF's decision. It is breathtakingly dishonest for the CDF to maintain its position is based "on the written Word of God" when Ratzinger knew full well that in 1976 the Pontifical Biblical Commission concluded unanimously that "the New Testament by itself alone" would not permit its members to settle "in a clear way and once for all" the question of women's ordination. The members of the Commission went further and supported the view that Scripture does not exclude the ordination of women and that to ordain women would not be against the intentions of Jesus.

This contemporary issue probably more than any other in the Catholic Church today reveals the arrogance, the dishonesty and the CDF's abuse of power as it uses doctrine to ensure no one questions how it wants the Church to operate.

The CDF's unquestioned authority in the name of protecting doctrine enables it to silence or dismiss from office any Catholic bishop, priest or theologian who dares to publicly support the ordination of women. Any public discussion of the issue is absolutely forbidden. Yet, beneath the theological mindset that professes to know with certainty the mind of God and of "Christ" on this issue is the reality that Jesus did not start a new religion with its own priesthood. Instead, he called for wholehearted commitment to his dream for a better humanity, a dream he was ready to die for.

It is hard to imagine Jesus thinking that women had a lesser role than men to play in gathering the community into commitment to his dream.

It is time to focus on the human reality of Jesus the dreamer the night before he died if we are to understand and put into operation how a community gathering in remembrance of him might exercise leadership and perform ritual.

11

....

GOOD FRIDAY. FAITH

Paul's understanding of "the Christ" and the worldview in which he envisioned "the Christ" operating became the basis for Christian doctrine about the death of Jesus.

It is time to question that this is the only way Jesus' death can be viewed. It is time to question the insistence of Joseph Ratzinger, the *Catechism of the Catholic Church*, the CDF and the Magisterium of the Catholic Church that Jesus' death "must be believed and taught" as "a sacrificial offering to the Father for the forgiveness of sins". In 2005, to further emphasize this stance, the CDF issued a statement alerting Roman Catholic theologians they were not to cast doubt on the proposition that "Jesus accepted to suffer punishment for our sins or to die to satisfy the justice of God."

This is held up as doctrine never to be questioned.

And where did this doctrine come from?

It did not come from Jesus. Jesus would surely have been hor-
rified that anyone would change his notion of a loving and
compassionate God into a deity who required a price to be paid
before granting forgiveness. He made clear in his parables that
his notion of God's extravagant forgiveness and graciousness
exceeded any human concepts of justice.

The doctrine came from Paul and his notion of "the Christ"
winning access to the heavenly home of God. It was Paul who
taught that the world was essentially sinful because of Adam's
fall. It was Paul who cemented the belief that there was no possibility of forgiveness from God without Jesus dying for the sins
of humanity. It was Paul who preached that Jesus "was handed
over to death for our trespasses and was raised for our justifica-
tion." (Romans 4:25) It came from Paul who transformed Jesus
into a semi-god acceptable to the Greek-Roman world.

We are not allowed to question the doctrine because Paul's writing is considered the "very voice of God who cannot lie", and
doctrine based on Paul has been elevated to the same status.

What would happen if we, as faithful followers of Jesus, were to
defy the Pope, the CDF, the *Catechism of the Catholic Church*
and the Magisterium of the Church, and openly question, even
reject, Paul's thinking about Jesus' death and the doctrine that
goes with it?

We would meet Jesus as he would want us to meet him. He
would be real, rather than a theological construct with little

resemblance to the Jewish man who preached the urgent need to establish the kingdom of God on earth. We would encounter a deeply inspiring and courageous man. We would engage a story that reveals the depth of the Divine Presence in the human, in Jesus and in each of us.

Jesus did not believe he had to die in order to win God's forgiveness. We only have to read his parables about God's mercy to know he did not believe in a vengeful God or a God who dispensed justice as our sins deserved. The wayward son, for example, would have had to work in the fields for many, many years before the father could have forgiven him if Jesus thought God acted according to our human measures of justice. And Jesus certainly would not have told people to walk in a relationship of utter trust with God, if he believed God was withholding forgiveness from people because of Adam's sin.

We have to look elsewhere, beyond the warped notion of a God who required Jesus to "accept to suffer punishment for our sins or to die to satisfy the justice of God" if we are to find the true significance of Jesus' death and its importance to us.

Jesus died a shameful death on a cross because that was where his life and his preaching took him. He accepted the consequences of what he stood for. He did not see himself as a grandiose, other-worldly "Christ" figure striding the heavens and the earth, setting everything right between God and sinful humanity. He was a courageous Jewish man who gave the best possible human expression he could to the gracious, life-giving, compassionate, Divine Presence within him. He lived in integrity to the fullest extent possible. He did what many others have done and continue to do: he stood up for what he believed and accepted the consequences. His final journey to Jerusalem was precisely that: this is where I stand; this is what I am ready to die for.

The human condition and human systems of control and governance led Jesus to his death, not a God ruling from the heavens. Life took Jesus and tested him. The faith questions we face whenever life really tests us are questions such as, "What do you believe now about God and goodness when life does this to you? What are you pinning your hopes on now?" Our life experience often teaches us that trust in the basic goodness of reality and faith in a Divine Presence with us are not easy when we encounter tragedy, pain, failure, loneliness or emotional hardship. In such times, our Christian faith should lead us instinctively to Jesus with the certainty that he knows the human condition, that our hearts can touch, and we can draw strength and hope and inspiration from his courage and integrity.

We are told in the gospels that Jesus taught "with authority". We can presume that this was not the sort of authority the temple priests and the "legal experts from Jerusalem" exercised, but the authority of someone who lived what he preached. This was a man who *knew* the pains and struggles of the human condition. He demonstrated in his own pain and struggle that it was possible to hold onto belief in the utter goodness and graciousness of God, and to trust in the presence of God, whatever the darkness.

This is the Jesus we need to contemplate on Good Friday, not the unreal semi-god figure of doctrine whose divine will steadfastly held all human emotion in check and preserved Jesus from any struggle of faith as he fulfilled the outrageous demands of an offended deity in the heavens.

How could Christianity have constructed doctrine that required Jesus to have a divine will that removed from him the need to live by faith and trust the way the rest of humanity does? The answer is obvious. It happened because Christianity elevated Paul's Christology above fidelity to Jesus' humanity and his message about life here on earth.

Jesus, the human expression of the Divine, invites us to hold onto the faith in which he confronted his terrible death. We should contemplate the manner of his dying as a supreme act of faith in God in the midst of suffering and loneliness. Jesus on the cross has every right to ask us to look him in the eye and to give our word that we will live in the faith in which he was prepared to die.

The Jesus of the CDF, "the Christ" with a divine will who knew all things with certainty and did not need to live by faith the way we do, has no right, no "authority" to ask this of us. This theological construct does not know our struggles; he is play-acting his way through life and death.

Should we be surprised that so many Christians in times of struggle do not turn to Jesus because they believe and say, "He was God, He would not understand what I am going through."

Doctrine might say Jesus was fully human as well as fully divine, but the reality is that the doctrine is playing with words under the guise of mystery "beyond human understanding". Jesus was only human in this doctrinal construct to the extent he had a human body with feelings. Beyond that, the doctrinal Jesus, the Christ of Paul, had nothing in common with us. He did not share with us our human need to search, to question, to work through doubts, to grow in understanding, to be enlightened, to feel powerless, to wonder what the future holds, to agonize over decisions to be made, and to wonder if the right decision has been made. He did not have to confront death with any uncertainty about what lay beyond. No, the divine will took care of all that.

What *has* doctrine done to Jesus!

There is another lamentable effect of doctrine about Jesus. By turning Jesus into "the Christ", and from there into being "consubstantial with the Father", Christianity lost sight of one of the most important insights to be gleaned from Good Friday. It is an insight based on everything Jesus preached and was ready to die for: the belief that the Divine Presence is in all people.

Jesus' insight about the here and now reality of the Divine Presence in people is missed when we contemplate his death as someone utterly unlike us who died to set things right with God. It is only when we contemplate the human reality of Jesus on the cross, someone faithful to his vision despite all the pain and struggle, that his life-giving and inspiring insight is able to dawn in our awareness. We contemplate his integrity, his courage, and his faithfulness. We contemplate the depth of the Spirit of God in this man. We honor the reality that Jesus was human like us, then the Aha! moment comes! This Spirit of God in Jesus is the *very same* Spirit active in our lives when we struggle to be good, to be courageous, to take a stand, to bear suffering and disappointments, to be faithful to what we know to be true and loving.

Jesus' manner of dying reveals the extraordinary capacity of the human to rise above evil and pain and struggle and fears. And Jesus would surely want us to "see" this, and to draw hope from it. He would doubtless invite us to look around among our friends and relatives, and see where this same Spirit of the Divine has emerged in wondrous and surprising ways in their courage, integrity and fidelity.

We would find evidence of this courage in people all around the world. Jesus would invite us to contemplate this phenomenon of human existence. "Look," he would say, "the very same Spirit you profess to be in me is in all of you. Deepen your awareness of this Presence in you and know it can do far more than you can ask or imagine. Use the Presence within and among you to work for a better world."

Doctrine about Jesus with two natures does not lead us to this Jesus or to the insight about the depth of the Divine Spirit in the human.

It never has. It never will.

12

....

R E S U R R E C T I O N .
T R A N S F O R M A T I O N

On the occasion of the hundredth anniversary of the founding of
the Pontifical Biblical Commission, Joseph Ratzinger, then head
of the CDF, delivered a speech on the relationship between the
teaching authority of the Church and scripture scholars. In the
speech he effectively obliged Catholic scripture scholars to stay
within doctrine based on scripture's understanding of a heavenly
interventionist deity:

> A God who cannot intervene in history and reveal
> Himself is not the God of the Bible. In this way the
> reality of the birth of Jesus by the Virgin Mary, the
> effective institution of the Eucharist by Jesus at the
> Last Supper, his bodily resurrection from the dead -
> this is the meaning of the empty tomb - are elements
> of faith as such, which it can and must defend against
> an only presumably superior historical knowledge.

That Jesus - in all that is essential - was effectively who the Gospels reveal him to be to us is not mere historical conjecture, but a fact of faith.

With this notion of God firmly established, any reflection on or teaching about the resurrection of Jesus is simple. You believe the stories in the Gospels. You believe that Jesus was physically raised from the dead, that he had meals with his friends, that people could touch his wounded body, and that forty days after he was raised from death, he physically rose from the earth and journeyed somewhere into space to reach God's dwelling place in the sky.

There is a far better way to attend to the resurrection stories in the gospels. It does not conflict with twenty-first century knowledge about the physical laws of the universe as traditional doctrine does. It does not involve the interventionist activity of an elsewhere deity. It attends to the stories in the context of the Divine Presence everywhere. The stories will still have a clear, hopeful message for us. They tell us, as they were intended to tell people two thousand years ago, that, yes, Jesus died, but in some way he lives on beyond death. They tell us, as they told people then, that Jesus is now fully embraced in the Divine, yet in some way he is still with us. They tell us that beyond death are transformation and communion with the Divine that are beyond our human imagination.

The resurrection stories convey to us the good news that living in love and giving human expression to the Divine Presence has a dimension that will outlast our human reality. Death will not be the end, but a continuation of the connection we already have with the Divine in our humanity. Living in love and living in the Divine Presence is never ending. Jesus was not the cause of this good news. It did not start with him. This was always true of humanity. It was a major mistake for Paul and for formal Christian teaching to tell people otherwise.

Doctrinal certainty based on a literal understanding of gospel stories about the risen Jesus being taken up into heaven and reconnecting humanity with an elsewhere God can no longer be beyond questioning. The questions include:

Will we continue to interpret whatever happened to Jesus when he died in the understanding that no one who died before Jesus entered into a transformative communion with the Divine Presence in death?

How do we think about death today? Do we think of it as a journey to an elsewhere place (heaven) where we will meet God? Or does our knowledge of consciousness and our understanding that energy is all-pervasive lead us into a different understanding, however tentative and speculative that might be?

Paul made the resurrection of Jesus foundational in his understanding of "the Christ". He believed and taught that if God had not taken Jesus up into heaven we would still be "dead" in our sins, with no hope of being set right with God. (1 Corinthians 15:16-19)

The word of God as expressed by Paul can be sadly mistaken if it implies that people the world over who lived before Jesus had no communion with the Divine Presence when they died.

Following Paul's line of thinking, Christian doctrine presented the resurrection of Jesus as the "big bang" of religious experience. We are meant to believe that before Jesus was "taken up into heaven" no one who lived before him had access to transformative communion with the Divine Presence when they died. We were taught that everyone who died before Jesus went to a shadowy holding place, somewhere below the earth. Jesus "descended there" before the heavenly God raised him.

It is time for Christians to explore the notion of God that drives this thinking.

It is time to start asking where this notion about all the dead being locked out of heaven came from. It did not come from Jesus. It did not come from the earliest preaching about "the Way" of Jesus.

We all know it came from literalizing the story of Adam and Eve's fall. Not surprisingly, the *Catechism of the Catholic Church*, while conceding that the story "uses figurative language", insists that the story "affirms a primeval event, a deed that took place at the beginning of the history of man." (#930)

Here, the Magisterium of the Catholic Church has to disregard the scholarship of its own Pontifical Biblical Commission about not taking the Genesis story literally. It has to depend on its insistence that "the word of God cannot lie". It has to disregard all the available scientific evidence pointing to the fact that the human species did not emerge from a state of paradise. It has to engage in this fantasy in order to defend its doctrines about original sin , about "the Christ" who "saved" us, about Jesus having to be a unique incarnation of a heavenly deity in order to accomplish this "salvation", about Jesus with a divine and a human nature, about Jesus' death being a sacrificial act on his part to win forgiveness for humanity's sins, about his resurrection from the dead being a physical reality, about "the Christ" being consubstantial with the Father, about God being a Trinity of persons, and of course, about the Church being founded by God Himself.

It is time to reject the presumptions and the notion of God and the interpretation of scriptural stories on which all those doctrines depend. Humanity was never, and could never be, cut off from the Divine Presence.

It is time to consider Jesus' resurrection not in terms of a journey to an overseeing, heavenly God who had disconnected from humanity, but as a transformation from being a human expression of the Divine to living on in the Divine beyond all human limits. It is time to see that "resurrection" will be ours also. It is time to see that "resurrection" in this contemporary understanding did not start with Jesus. The human species has always lived in and died into the Divine Presence.

It is time to appreciate that Christianity as a religion will not crumble and fall if Jesus' death and resurrection are interpreted in a radically different way from the understanding of Paul, traditional Christian doctrine and the teaching of the Magisterium.

It is time to insist that faith be built on sound reasoning, on sound data, and on sound scriptural scholarship rather than on doctrines based on a literal understanding of a fall at humanity's beginning and driven by notions of an elsewhere, interventionist God.

As twenty-first century Christians we can continue to gather around the mythical stories concerning Jesus' resurrection. While we acknowledge the very different cultural and scientific paradigms in which they were written, we value them for the wisdom they contain. We appreciate them as stories honoring Jesus' fidelity to what he believed. We respect them because they point us to the mystery of life after death. These stories lead us to believe that, like Jesus, we, too, live in and will die into the Divine Presence.

It is time to bring to these stories our contemporary understanding of the universe, our searching questions about consciousness and energy, and our belief in an all-pervasive Divine Presence. In this context the stories can have profound meaning, whereas interpreted literally and encased in doctrinal certitude, they will be rejected as pre-scientific make-believe, with no wisdom or insight to offer.

....

13

THE UNREALITY OF DOCTRINE.
MARY, THE MOTHER OF JESUS.

Among the doctrines that Roman Catholic scripture scholars and theologians are forbidden to question publicly are those concerning Mary, the mother of Jesus. They include doctrines about the "immaculate conception" of Mary, the virginal conception of Jesus, and Mary's bodily "assumption" into heaven.

These doctrines assume that Mary knew she had been chosen by God to be the mother of "the Christ" and acted accordingly.

The problem is that this understanding did not emerge until about fifty years after Jesus died. There is no reference to it until the infancy accounts in the gospels of Luke and Matthew. Mark has no "special birth" story for Jesus. It would appear that Paul knew of no such story either.

Mark's treatment of Mary is of particular significance. He has only three references to Mary, and none of them are very flattering. He does not present her as "blessed among women" or knowing her son was "the Christ".

In his first reference, Mark records that Jesus went to a house and such a crowd gathered that he and his followers were unable to eat:

> When his family heard what was happening, they came to take control of him. They were saying, "He's out of his mind!" (3:20)

Jesus' "*family*", not distant relatives, thought he was insane and needed to be taken away and controlled. In Mark's gospel, Jesus' own family members were at the forefront of people who did not understand that he was "the Christ", God's beloved Son. If we surmise that Mary participated in this "family" event, then we are led to conclude that she, too, misunderstood Jesus and what he was doing. This conclusion would be impossible to hold if we are guided by Matthew and Luke's infancy accounts which indicate that Mary knew who her child really was. Mark, however, appears to know nothing of these accounts and would seem to include Mary among the family members who did not understand Jesus.

His second reference to Mary comes in the same chapter as he continues the theme of misunderstanding. He records how the "legal experts from Jerusalem" came and accused Jesus of doing the work of the devil. Not only was Jesus at odds with his family but also with the religious legal authorities. In an apparent response to his family and the religious authorities, Jesus gives a speech about the dangers of "a kingdom divided" and he warns against "insulting the Holy Spirit" with accusations that he is doing the work of the devil. In this setting, Mark then relates:

> His mother and his brothers arrived. They stood outside and sent word to him, calling for him. A crowd was seated around him and the messengers said, "Look, your mother, brothers and sisters are outside looking for you." And he replied, "Who is my mother? Who are my brothers?" Looking around at those seated with him in a circle, he said, "Look, here are my mother and my brothers. Whoever does God's will is my brother, sister and mother." (3:31-35)

Here, Mark makes it clear that not only did Mary not understand Jesus, but that Jesus dismissed her because of her lack of understanding.

Mary does not appear again in Mark's Gospel, except for an indirect reference to her in chapter 6 when Jesus returned to Nazareth and preached in the synagogue:

> Many who heard him were surprised. "Where did this man get all this? What is the wisdom he's been given? What about the powerful acts accomplished through him? Isn't this the carpenter? Isn't he Mary's son and the brother of James, Joses, Judas and Simon? Aren't

his sisters here with us?" They were repulsed by him
and fell into sin.

Jesus said to them, "Prophets are honored everywhere
except in their own hometown, among their relatives,
and in their own households."... He was appalled by
their disbelief. (6:1-6)

According to Mark, Jesus found no honor from his own relatives
and from anyone within his "own household".

If the Magisterium of the Catholic Church relied on Mark as
the primary gospel source, it is highly unlikely it would have
concluded that Mary had to be immaculately conceived, that
she deserved to be assumed body and soul into heaven and now
enjoys Queen of Heaven status. The author of Mark's gospel
would surely wonder how the Church could arrive at such an
understanding about the Mary in his gospel.

The fact is that the Church conveniently overlooked Mark's
view of Mary in favor of the infancy stories in Matthew and
Luke. These appeared about a decade after Mark. The stories
include dreams and annunciations and angels rejoicing about
this child who was born without the aid of a human father. Mary
is extolled as truly blessed and in Luke's gospel gives voice to
the wonderful "Magnificat".

There was a "knowing" then of just who this child was. In Luke's
gospel, for example, Simeon rejoiced because he had been told

"by the Holy Spirit that he should not see death before he had seen the Lord's Christ." Over the centuries, these gospel stories established in the minds of those who read or heard them that Mary knew, even before the birth, that her child was to be "the Christ". Christians generally came to believe that the miraculous details surrounding Jesus' birth are factual, a part of "gospel truth".

In reality, this is another instance of Paul's Christology being written back into Jesus' life, and in the process creating a totally unreal picture of what might have happened. Although, we will never know what really happened before, during and after Jesus' birth, we can be reasonably sure that it was nothing like the infancy accounts we have in these two Gospels.

Biblical scholars can provide us with the background information we need to explain how, when and why Mary was transformed from disbeliever in Mark's gospel to the privileged status of a virginal mother who knew her son was "the Lord's Christ" in Matthew and Luke. The scholars point us to the Greek and Roman "mystery religions" of those times. Those religions told stories of semi-god heroes who were born from the union of a god with a woman, had conquered the forces of evil and had gained access to the heavenly realm. Once Paul's preaching locked Jesus into gaining access to the heavenly realm, it was only a matter of time before stories arose about his birth that gave him equal status with those other semi-gods or with Caesar

Augustus whose birth received similar embellishment not long after he died.

Without a special birth, Jesus would have been outranked by the semi-gods of Greek and Roman mystery religions. He would lack credibility as a cosmic figure. The stories of his miraculous conception and birth appeared sometime after Paul died in order to support Paul's transformation of Jesus into "the Christ". The stories have no basis in reality. They are not historical; they are not factual. Scholars know they are mythical accounts and are not meant to be taken literally. They are part of "the Christ" myth. The scholars, however, are forbidden to use their knowledge to question the truth of doctrinal statements about the "virgin Mary".

According to Joseph Ratzinger, the CDF and Roman Catholic tradition the doctrinal statements about Mary are factual. They are absolute truth, "more certain than all human knowledge". They must "be believed and taught".

The fact is that faith based on Marian doctrine is not certain. We really have no idea of what the real Mary was like. If the *Catechism of the Catholic Church* believes that Mark's Gospel is "the very word of God that cannot lie", then it has to accept that Mark's Mary would dismally fail any canonization process.

The gospel transformation of Mary provides a clear illustration of how doctrine can oblige Catholics to believe something is absolute truth, the very word of God himself, when it is nothing of the kind. Doctrine grows out of interpretation. It grows out of stories. It is constructed within particular understandings of God and how this God is in relationship with the universe. Doctrines about Mary and about Jesus' birth arose from Paul's interpretation of the role of Jesus, from images and ideas that developed as a result of that interpretation, and from the understanding that God lived in the heavenly realms.

The problems with Marian doctrine highlight the difference between doctrine and story, or between doctrine and myth. The Church's insistence that doctrine is certain, unchangeable reality gives many Catholics little option except to reject the doctrine when what is being taught is clearly not factual. The pity is that the stories on which the doctrine is based are also dismissed as fantasy and as having nothing to offer the modern mind.

Story, however, can be like Jesus' use of parable. Story, as we saw with the resurrection of Jesus, invites people to see beyond the narrative and to be open to symbol, insights and meaning. The stories about Mary in the gospels can invite contemporary readers to reflect on the experience of the struggle to change from deeply ingrained religious beliefs and attitudes to a new way of understanding. Mary can still be held as a model for the Church community, not because she was immaculately conceived, but because she can be viewed as a woman who mirrors the struggle we all experience in shifting from a faith perspective we never thought we would question to a faith deeply committed to the dream of Jesus.

In a Church dominated by male control and an exclusively male-oriented theology about God and Church, many Catholics will continue to prefer devotion to Mary over a relationship with a punitive God and the unreal Jesus of Catholic theology. This is more about a search for a spirituality that touches peoples' hearts and experience than correct theological thinking. This search cannot be addressed by doctrine.

Some Christians will object that devotion to Mary elevates her to a status that is not credible in the modern world, and they have sound reasons for their objections. On the other hand, male institutional leadership in the Catholic Church has failed people with its focus on correct theological thinking. It has left them devoid of a wholesome spirituality that embraces the feminine, the heart, and intuition. It is not surprising that so many Catholics have looked to the stories about Mary in the gospels of Luke, Matthew and John to find what is lacking.

A challenge facing the Catholic Church is to address the unreality of doctrine and the excesses of Marian devotion. It can do this by being open to scriptural scholarship that demonstrates how to value and respect myth, narrative and story. It can do so by embracing the contemporary "universe story" and bringing to that story a basic Christian appreciation that the Divine Presence is everywhere. It can do it by acknowledging that Jesus and Mary and each one of us share the *same* wonderful story - we all give human expression to the Divine Presence. Jesus and Mary are more like us than institutional Christianity would ever have us imagine.

14

....

QUESTIONS ABOUT
THE COSMIC CHRIST

There is a stream of progressive Christian thought based on Paul, and often following Teilhard de Chardin, that frees itself from the fall-redemption story of salvation and promotes an understanding of a "cosmic Christ". Yet in some ways, this progressive thought is akin to putting new wine into old wineskins. Its proponents often articulate an understanding of "the Christ" within the framework of a "new story" about the universe and its origins and evolutionary development on earth but at the same time remain rooted, as de Chardin was, in classical, traditional Christological foundations.

Before we consider the Christology of de Chardin and his followers, let us reflect briefly on the man himself. His conflict with Church authorities sheds significant light on how the Vatican defends the unreality of doctrine despite evidence against it.

Teilhard de Chardin SJ was born in 1881 and died in 1955. His expertise and interest in paleontology, geology, evolution, and philosophy led him to consider the universe in the framework of constant evolutionary development. He noted that development unfolds in ever increasing complexity and consciousness. Like many evolutionary thinkers before him, de Chardin thought about the "jump" from matter to life. He concluded that all matter is endowed with "spirit", so there is no "jump". Rather, everything is part of "a coordinated system of activity which is gradually rising up toward freedom and consciousness." Matter, he wrote, "is spirit moving slowly enough to be seen." At the heart of this system are spirit, love, consciousness and co-operation. This is beautifully expressed in the well-known quote from his best-known book, *The Phenomenon of Man:*

Cosmic energy is love,

the affinity of Being with being.

It is a universal property of all life

and embraces all forms of organized matter.

Thus the tendency to unite;

the attraction of atom to atom;

molecule to molecule;

or cell to cell.

The forces of love

drive the fragments of the universe

to seek each other,

so that the world may come into being.

Teilhard dreamed of the day when "we shall harness for God the energies of love, and then, for a second time in the history of the world, man will have discovered fire." He believed that "the epic drama of evolution" would reach its conclusion when humans "individually and collectively will eventually enter into the ultimate, perfect union with God at the Omega Point".

In the 1920's de Chardin found himself in conflict with both Rome and his Jesuit superiors because his evolutionary thinking called into question the idea of a "fall" at the beginning of the human species. He was ordered to resign from his teaching position in France and required to sign a statement withdrawing his controversial statements about original sin. In 1944, Rome banned him from publishing *The Phenomenon of Man*. The ban was renewed in 1947 when Rome also forbade him to write about or to teach philosophy. In 1955 the "Supreme Authority of the Holy Office" decreed that none of de Chardin's works were to be sold in Catholic bookshops or to be translated into other languages.

Condemnation from Rome continued even after he died. In 1962, the "most eminent and most revered Fathers of the Holy Office" (as members of the CDF humbly called themselves in those days) issued an "exhortation" that bishops, religious superiors, and rectors of seminaries "protect the minds, particularly of the youth" against the dangers of de Chardin "and his followers".

The "most revered Fathers of the Holy Office" discerned enough from de Chardin's writings to believe that the basic evolutionary process he proposed clashed with the doctrine of original sin. It did not matter that de Chardin wrote eloquently about "the Christ" as the focal point of the evolutionary process. The Fathers of the Holy Office feared his thinking could lead readers to call into question the literal interpretation of the Adam and Eve story and the doctrine of original sin.

The teaching of the Magisterium on the origins of the human species was made eminently clear in 1950, when Pope Pius XII issued the Encyclical, *Humani Generis*. The encyclical set the limits for Catholic theologians on evolutionary thinking. It gave approval to study the emergence of the human in evolutionary terms "as far as it inquires into the origin of the human body as coming from pre-existent and living matter". However, no doubt was to be cast on the belief "that souls are immediately created by God."

Furthermore, anyone writing about evolution must be:

> "prepared to submit to the judgment of the Church,
> to whom Christ has given the mission of interpreting

authentically the Sacred Scriptures and of defending the dogmas of faithful." (#36)

Rome was making it very clear to everyone that the Church, not science, should and would have the final say or judgment on what constitutes reality.

The encyclical then gives another classic example of defending doctrine no matter what evidence there may be to the contrary:

> When, however, there is question of another conjectural opinion, namely polygenism, the children of the Church by no means enjoy such liberty. For the faithful cannot embrace that opinion which maintains that either after Adam there existed on this earth true men who did not take their origin through natural generation from him as from the first parent of all, or that Adam represents a certain number of first parents. It is no way apparent how such an opinion can be reconciled with that which the sources of revealed truth and the documents of the Teaching Authority of the Church propose with regard to original sin, which proceeds from a sin actually committed by an individual Adam and which through generation is passed on to all and is in everyone as his own. (#37)

The "sources of revealed truth and the documents of the Teaching Authority of the Church" override any scientific data.

Once again the teaching authority of the Catholic Church backed itself into a corner here. Having elevated its doctrinal teaching to the level of God's truth, it would lose face and credibility if it were to admit that any doctrine was constructed on erroneous or unreal foundations.

Today we are living through the continuation of, and what may well be the final phase of, this desperate and dishonest battle between the teaching authority of the Catholic Church and scientific evidence shaping our understanding of reality. The CDF resolutely demands unqualified assent to doctrinal conclusions while many thinking Catholics want to have open and honest dialogue about the data and processes on which those conclusions have been based. The CDF knows it cannot afford to allow such open, scholarly dialogue, and insists instead that the only options are to give assent to, or to dissent from, the teaching authority of the Church in its doctrinal statements.

Like scholars today, Teilhard de Chardin knew he was never going to win his personal battle with the Magisterium. He never wanted to be at odds with Catholic teaching, though he had earlier found his religion disappointing because "it never developed the sense of the earth". However, his attitude to his faith changed when he came to believe that Paul's vision of the "universal Christ" could bring Christian faith and science together in wonderful harmony

As early as 1934, in his book, *How I Believe*, de Chardin outlined how the Pauline "Christ" had become central to his faith perspective. The risen "Christ" was the Omega point to which the universe, all freedom, all consciousness, all complexity, and human existence, was heading - or being drawn to by God. He wrote:

> It is, then, in this physical pole of universal evolution that we must, in my view, locate and recognize the plenitude of Christ.

> All I am doing (let me repeat) is to transpose into terms of physical reality the juridical expressions in which the Church has clothed her faith...

> I tried to place at the head of the universe which I adored from birth, the risen Christ whom others have taught me to know ... and I have never for the past twenty five years ceased to marvel at the infinite possibilities which the "universalization" of Christ opens up for religious thought...The world around me becomes divine...

> For, (and this is perhaps the most wonderful part of the whole story) the Universal Christ in whom my personal faith finds satisfaction, is none other than the authentic expression of the Christ of the Gospel...

The more I have thought about the magnificent cosmic attributes lavished by St Paul on the risen Christ … the more clearly have I realized that Christianity takes on its full value only when extended … to cosmic dimensions.

Thus, ahead of us, a universal cosmic center is taking on definition in which everything reaches its term, in which everything is explained, is felt, is ordered.

Later, in his last volume of essays written in 1950, *The Heart of the Matter*, Teilhard composed a prayer to the "Ever Greater Christ" which in part reads:

"You, by right of your resurrection, had assumed the dominating position of all-inclusive Center in which everything is gathered together."

Teilhard believed Paul's Christology "divinized" the universe and everything in it, and that the evident evolutionary processes were intimately connected with God's plan. This understanding gave progressive Christian thinkers, especially Roman Catholic academics, an alternate faith perspective to the fall-redemption model as they tried to reconcile Christian faith with the reality of "the new story of the universe".

There are, however, several major problems with "cosmic Christ" thinking, and, as with doctrine, it is time to bring them out into the open.

The first problem is the tendency to accept Paul's Christology as if it were reality. Paul's Christology is unreal. It is visionary. It is gratuitous. It is not scientific. It changed the reality of Jesus into something Jesus would never recognize. It is a radical departure from Jesus' understanding of the Divine Presence in peoples' lives. It changed Jesus' own concept of being "christos", called to preach the good news, into Paul's grandiose concept of "the Christ" who won access to heaven and gained forgiveness for sinful humanity.

A second problem is the use of the word "Christ" which has a particular meaning within both Judaism and Christianity. Unfortunately, in Christianity, the word is often used interchangeably with "Jesus". We commonly hear or read that "Christ" did this or that, when it is clear from the context that Jesus is being referred to. "Jesus Christ" has become Jesus' name for many Christians. Because "Christ" is so generally associated with Jesus, by Christians and non-Christians, it is problematic to use the word in the context of a new story about the universe where we want language, terminology and ideas that are universally acceptable. Cosmic "*Christ*" is too overlaid with Christian theology. It is too connected in peoples' minds with Jesus. The challenge is to stop using the word "Christ" and to articulate a story about the Divine Presence in the universe without reliance on Paul's Christology.

A third problem concerns Roman Catholic writers in particular. Like de Chardin, they are clearly restrained within doctrinal boundaries. For some, their teaching positions are dependent on not publicly dissenting from Church doctrine. Consequently, when reading their work, it is difficult to know whether they are writing with one eye on the CDF or whether what they write is really what they believe. Many Roman Catholic authors writing about the "cosmic Christ" and the "new story" clearly think they are breaking new theological ground. However, many hold onto some, if not most, of the following doctrinal notions:

1. The notion of a personal God who plans.

Cosmic Christ theology based on Paul consistently presumes belief in a heavenly deity who has a plan for the universe. Many writers about the Cosmic Christ envisage a God who has planned the unfolding of the universe with his "Christ" in mind. Some writers state that God's plan for the fulfillment of everything "in Christ" will not be thwarted. There is no data, no evidence, for this claim apart from trying to fit the new universe story into Paul's outmoded worldview and his notion of God who has eternal plans for humanity. A realistic twenty-first century cosmic theology will need to move well beyond the scriptural and doctrinal notion of God.

2. The uniqueness of the incarnation of Jesus.

Roman Catholic writers cannot write or say publicly anything that would cast doubt on established doctrine about Jesus being the incarnate Son of God who was "sent" down from heaven to fulfill God's plans to "save" humanity from the effects of original sin. Nor can they ignore the topic, so the incarnation is often mentioned as if the writer holds to the doctrine concerning the uniqueness of Jesus. However, their treatment inevitably raises doubts whether this is what they really believe or whether it is written to prevent any problems with Church authority. Writers cannot be held accountable for this state of affairs, but it illustrates how doctrinal rectitude holds back academic exploration. It is time, as we saw earlier, to appreciate that Jesus' role as revealer of the Divine in the context of "new story" does not require him to be the unique incarnation of a God who disconnected from this world.

3. The resurrection of Jesus ushered in a new relationship between humanity and God.

This understanding contradicts the ministry and preaching of Jesus. He firmly believed that living in love is intimately connected with living *in* God's goodness and graciousness. He did not initiate this connection. He articulated what he believed was always an essential aspect of human living and loving. It did not begin only after his death.

4. The risen Jesus, "the Christ", sent the Spirit of God from heaven.

There was no "sending" of the Spirit of God from the heavenly heights. The Divine Presence was always with people. Jesus believed so and wanted people to draw hope and strength from that Presence with them. After Jesus' death his followers gathered in his memory, told their stories about him, and committed themselves to carry on his dream. It was this gathering together that allowed the Divine Presence, always within and among them, to come to clear and strong expression in their thinking and acting. It is time to disassociate ourselves from notions of the "Spirit of God" being sent to earth from another place after Jesus died.

5. "The Christ" set humanity free from the bonds of sin and death.

It is time to ask whether Jesus envisioned a God who held people in "bonds". His preaching about God-with-us has the capacity to set us free from any "bondage" created by the realities of sin and death. It is not "the Christ" who did this and "set us free". It is Jesus, the "son of man", who showed by his life and teaching how all of us can live free of any such bondage. His way of life was well established in preaching and living before Paul decided that freedom only came through faith in the risen Jesus, "the Christ".

6. Eternal life with God is God's gift to us through, and only through, "the Christ".

This belief rests on a literal understanding of the Adam and Eve story and the idea that God reacted to Adam and Eve's wrongdoing by closing off access to his heavenly home. Apart from such literalization, there is not the slightest evidence to suggest that people who died before Jesus did not die into communion with the Divine Presence. It is time to discard the belief that eternal life with God only began with the raising of Jesus into heaven.

7. Elevating the resurrection and Paul's theology over the life and preaching of Jesus.

Too many writers give lip-service to Jesus' life and ministry, while maintaining that the resurrection was the really important event, having cosmic consequences that overshadow the earthly existence of Jesus. It is time to place the earthly, truly human Jesus and his urgent message about human conduct at the very center of the Christian religion.

It would be regrettable if Catholic and other Christian writers thought "cosmic Christ" thinking was the best or the only way to rescue Jesus from the fall-redemption theology, and so make him relevant to contemporary cosmology and its questions about "God". It is not the only way and it is far from being the best way.

A much better way would be to rescue Jesus from Paul's Christology altogether and to see him, as expressed throughout this book, as a human expression of the Divine Presence at work in the universe. We should engage him as friend and companion who reveals the Divine in each of us. This engagement would lead to the rightful focus on his teaching about establishing the influence of the Divine Presence in all human interactions. It is this personal knowing of Jesus that will lead people to move beyond the constraints of doctrine and make Christianity relevant to the modern world.

15

....

THE WAY AHEAD

In recent years, episcopal control - it cannot be called leadership - in the Catholic Church has been characterized by oppression of any thinking that does not conform to the *Catechism
of the Catholic Church*. The system for selecting bishops
inherently rejects any candidate who has not demonstrated
strict adherence to the ecclesial system of thought control. As
a result, "Yes" men have risen to the surface. These men are
at home with the absolute power their position grants them.
They seem to have little problem with living as "princes of
the Church" and ruling over people. Quite a number of them
would be discounted as candidates for the office if fidelity
to living the Beatitudes ranked highly among the criteria for
selecting bishops. The Vatican, however, has no interest in the
Beatitudes when it comes to appointing bishops. It wants men
who will unquestioningly do the work the Vatican wants them
to do. There will be no public questioning of Catholic doctrine
with these men in position.

Concern to protect the theology that enshrines and protects the institution's claim to be founded by God himself and safeguarded from all error by God may seem a holy cause for these men and for many Catholics. In reality, the rigorous protection of doctrine at any cost reveals a sick institutional Church. The sickness has been manifested in recent years throughout the sexual abuse crisis. People around the world were shocked to hear cardinals, archbishops and bishops callously disregard the gospel call to mourn with and to show empathy toward victims, and see them choose instead to protect the Church's "good name" with secrecy, intimidation and denial. This was not and is not a healthy institution.

The mishandling of the sexual abuse scandal parallels the Vatican's systemic control over theological thinking. The same sick patterns are clear for all to see: paranoia, fear, suspicion, denial, refusal to accept evidence, secrecy, abuse of power, and protection of the institution at all costs. Institutional leadership with its system of governance in the Catholic Church today is intellectually bankrupt and morally corrupt.

We wait and expect to hear voices raised in protest. We know the voices are there. There are many of them. We have heard them privately. The public silence, however, is deafening. Very few dare to speak loudly. Very few dare to organize the voices into open dissent.

Is this not in itself a sign of the sickness of this Church? We dare not raise our voices? We dare not express that we no longer believe the theological "story" Rome and the CDF and the

Catechism demand we believe? We dare not seek dialogue about the foundations of our faith?

There are voices among the clergy, among scholars, among the members of religious congregations, and among many, many other Catholics. And everyone is warned by the CDF, "You will not raise your voices. There is only one voice to be heard, and that is the voice that agrees with what we determine is absolute, certain truth - the doctrine of the faith."

So the voices are not raised.

While many people will endorse the suppression, the sad reality is that the Roman Catholic Church, institutionally, is revealed to the world as closed-minded, oppressive, and fearful. It is not only incapable of making Jesus and his message relevant to the modern world, it does not live by the message of Jesus.

Many Roman Catholics, perhaps a majority, would have no knowledge of and no concern about this grievous situation. Parish community life is generally untouched by wider ecclesial issues. At the parish level, Church concerns are closer to home, such as why the younger generation does not go to Mass. Most Catholics are yet to see - or even hear - details of the massive theological shift facing all formal religions. They are yet to understand why their children and grandchildren have moved on from the notion of God and the story of "salvation" that ground Catholic faith. They are yet to understand that their children and grandchildren take a fundamentally different path from formal religion to arrive at an understanding of the Divine Presence, of the sacredness of the world in which they live, of their connection with all people, and of their own sacredness. A lengthy educational process is needed if adult Christians are to appreciate the enormity of the shift in religious thinking, but the institutional Church will not provide it if it entails questioning anything the *Catechism of the Catholic Church* teaches.

How can people who are aware of the theological shift and have been led to articulate their faith in new and more meaningful ways, sustain, develop and ritualize their faith in the midst of the crisis in which they find themselves? Is the parish community the place to do it? Many Catholics in this situation find themselves torn between loyalty to the parish faith community to which they have always belonged and the reality that the parish expression of faith neither nurtures their faith development nor ritualizes what they now believe.

The best response for some of these Catholics may be to stop attending Sunday Mass. Others might continue going to Mass, but will need to be very clear about the value for which they go. By clarifying the value for which they keep attending, they may be able to bring some balance to the frustration and disappointment they feel week after week when the liturgy does not harmonize with their faith journey.

Many men and women in Catholic religious congregations experience tension within their own congregations. While some members want to articulate and ritualize their faith within the parameters of a "new story", they are in community with others who remain loyal to traditional beliefs and expressions of Catholic faith. The need here may be to clarify, with great respect for one another, the inevitable differences in expectation about community prayer and liturgy when members of the same community are earnestly living out of different "stories" about God, Jesus, and Church.

This same tension exists in families and among friends within parish communities. The spirit of the Beatitudes challenges all Christians not to take up hardline positions, especially those that reject or disparage others. We are all challenged to tolerance, to empathy, to appreciation of differences, to respect. Perhaps the best attitude is to acknowledge that while we may be miles apart theologically, we agree not to let that drive a wedge between us. Deeply shared values, such as integrity, love and respect, can and should overcome any theological differences that may exist within families and communities and among friends.

Many Roman Catholics who are aware of the enormous shift in theological thought have given considerable time and effort to renewal movements in the Church, only to see their enthusiasm for reform deadened by intractable institutional resistance. Some continue their efforts, but many others have stopped trying to reform the institution. They put their energy into movements where they see possibilities for their faith to be nourished and ritualized.

The most significant "Church" movement in Roman Catholicism today is away from the institutional structures, away from systems of control, away from remote, centralized, clerical, dogmatic control over liturgy, and towards small faith-sharing communities where adult faith can be shared, nurtured, challenged and ritualized. Members of these small communities prefer to give time and effort to creating the "Church" they want to experience. Some hope that in years to come the institution may catch up with where the Divine Presence is presently leading people. For them, Jesus' parable about sowing seed is apt. Sow seed on fertile ground where growth is possible. Do not waste it on rocky ground or where thistles and weeds will strangle its growth.

The movement to small faith sharing communities is not without its own pitfalls, frustrations and disappointments. Sometimes this is because the group itself has never clearly articulated its purpose, and as a result becomes entangled in trying to fulfill the widely differing expectations of its members. This may happen when some members of the group want the group to explore new thinking and new forms of ritual while other members who have come to the group out of disillusionment with "the Church" may have no interest in exploring theology or participating in liturgy that is different from what "the Church" provided. They just want to get away from "the Church", while holding onto conventional faith beliefs. Consequently, some group members think or feel they have to refrain from openly sharing what they believe for fear of offending those with more traditional beliefs. Such a situation could be avoided if the group clearly articulated its purpose.

The following topics are offered for reflection and discussion by members of any small faith-sharing group interested in establishing a "church" experience that gives expression to the profound theological shift in which they find themselves.

1. Purpose of the group.

Is everyone in the group clear about the intentionality and purpose of the group? Do the group members have some familiarity with writers and speakers who are addressing the shift in which they find themselves? If not, will the group provide the members with further exposure to progressive thinking? Do group members want and expect to celebrate Christian ritual in ways that resonate with this thinking? How are individual group members challenged to take responsibility for the life of the group in whatever way they can?

2. Prayer.

Members of small faith groups who engage a more expansive notion of "God" may find themselves struggling to move beyond familiar language and prayer forms. It is very common to find progressive Christians who say they no longer believe in the notion of "God" being a listening deity, yet their vocal and liturgical prayers still address "God" as if this "God" were listening. The pattern of prayer addressed "to God" is deeply embedded deep in all of us. It is what we are familiar with, so we are unsure how to pray in any other way. Despite this, there are many people who no longer want to pray "to God", but are unsure how to pray otherwise. What to do?

As a starting point we should keep in mind that it is not necessary or even advisable to completely avoid prayer forms addressed "to God". Rather, it is a case of becoming more aware that this type of prayer is metaphor or personification. The prayer is not for the sake of a personal God who requires us to address "him" or "you". The Divine Presence has no need of our prayers. Nor is prayer about trying to change how this God acts. Prayer that addresses God is a way to give expression to the thoughts, feelings, reactions and longings within us. This prayer is always for our sakes, not for the sake of a God who hears.

The theological shift in which we find ourselves invites us to believe that everything and everyone is bonded with the Divine Presence, here, now. Accordingly, our prayer should give expression to this belief. We can do this by affirming the Presence here with us rather than using prayer forms that suggest we are addressing an elsewhere God. For example, a gathering prayer at the start of a gathering could be expressed in this way:

> As we gather today, let us be aware of the Divine
> Presence within and among us. We give thanks for

our awareness of this Presence, creatively active in all places at all times in the universe, and here today in our own lives. We open ourselves to this Presence that it may stir freely in our minds and hearts as it has stirred in so many people before us. Let us give this Divine Presence the best possible human expression we can in all that we do and say in our gathering. To this we give our Amen. *Amen.*

Making the effort to create new prayer forms can help us move beyond the familiar theological paradigm of an elsewhere God who needs our prayers, who listens to and sometimes responds to them. It can deepen our awareness of and appreciation for the Divine Presence in every aspect of our lives.

3. "God".

Another important aspect of our changing theological understanding is the word, "God". The word is too connected with a deity in heaven, the very notion we are trying to move away from, so why do we keep using it? Our conversations, our discussions and our prayer should try to move beyond the language and notions contained in doctrine. We should try to move them beyond identifying the Divine Presence with a god. Let us experiment with words that not only point us to this Mystery but also help to expand our understanding that this Mystery is everywhere. Throughout this book, "Divine Presence" has been used, but Divine, Creative, Energizing Presence also comes to mind, along with Ground of All That Exists, Sustainer of All, The All, The One, Awesome Mystery. Capital letters seem to help! Whatever names or words we use, it is not lost on listeners that we are trying to move beyond "God" language. Listeners have an understanding of the reality we are trying to point to with our words, and that is what is important.

4. Jesus and "Christ"

Likewise, let us stop using the word "Christ" as if it were Jesus' name. This will not come easily, but it is a discipline we need to engage if we are to deepen our awareness that Jesus, not "Christ" is the real heart and soul of Christian faith. The word *Christ* is misleading because it takes us away from Jesus and into institutional theology that is time and culturally conditioned. Jesus would not recognize or identity himself with "the Christ" of Paul's theology.

If we focus on *Jesus*, we focus on a human reality, on human experience, and the insights of someone living that experience. We can then bring that reality, experience and the insights to our living and our questioning today. To focus on Jesus affirms the Divine Presence within all of humanity and challenges everyone to give the best possible human expression to that Divine Presence. To focus on Jesus is open-ended. Being right or wrong, theologically, is not the issue. The issue is how to live lives that give clear expression to the Divine within all of us.

5. "Christian".

Can we continue to call ourselves "Christian" if we question and discard elements of doctrinal belief, especially those linked with Paul's understanding of "the Christ"? Yes, we can, if we faithfully understand "christos" in accordance with how Jesus, "the human one", understood his call or role. If we appropriate "christos" to ourselves in this way and choose to call ourselves "Christian", we can do so in awareness that the Spirit of the Lord, the Divine Presence, is upon us and that we are being prompted by this Presence to continue Jesus' dream and help establish "the kingdom of God" for the good of humanity and the earth.

6. Mission.

Some people expect a faith-sharing group to have a "mission", to be actively involved in a project or outreach. That need not be the case. Many members of small faith-sharing groups are already very active in various forms of social action. Gathering with the group to be "church" helps to nurture and develop their faith, while supporting them in the generosity of their busy lives. They do not need the group to set up another "mission" and expect them to be involved. On the other hand, some group members will find much benefit in bonding with and being supported by like-minded people as they engage in social action determined by the group or by some of its members.

7. Faith that is grounded.

As we challenge doctrines of the faith we must articulate the beliefs which will ground our religious faith today. It is not enough to proclaim what we no longer believe. We need to be clear about what we now believe and are committed to living. The following statements of belief may serve as a framework for group discussion and to help members of a group articulate reasonable, adult Christian faith for these times.

We acknowledge:

- that the Divine Presence is always present and active. It is never absent. It permeates everything that exists.

- that this mystery is beyond our human notions of "person" and the way we humans observe, react, think, plan and intervene.

- that the universality of consciousness and energy are worthwhile contemporary pointers to this Divine Presence permeating and sustaining everything that exists.

- that the Divine Presence is manifested in our universe and in our world through natural and observable patterns such as co-operation and the interconnection of everything that exists.

- that the human species emerged within the Divine Presence at work through these patterns.

- that the Divine Presence has been, is, and always will be, present within the human endeavor, as with everything that exists.

- that revelation comes from the ground up, from within the human community and all that exists, not from heaven down.

- that the Divine Presence is *naturally* given wonderful expression within the human community. The Divine Presence has manifested itself clearly in men and women throughout the ages who stress the need to work together, to co-operate with one another, to avoid violence and selfishness, and to care for one another. The Divine Presence manifests itself clearly in humanity in song, art, poetry, speech, wonder, love, and other forms of human creativity.

- that Jesus came from the Divine Presence here on earth – not from a God in the heavens.

- that Jesus understood how men and women might recognize the Divine Presence in their lives and give it the best possible human expression.

- it is the *message* of Jesus that is of paramount importance and must be heard.

- that when he died, Jesus died into the ebb and flow of the all-pervasive Divine Presence.

- that in calling ourselves "Christian" we will respond, as Jesus did, to the Divine Presence within and among us prompting us to work for a better world.

What we acknowledge and affirm will shape how we gather as "ecclesia", so we need to be clear about our beliefs, the purpose of the group, what we want to explore, and how we want to ritualize our commitment to being "ecclesia.

To be "ecclesia" involves gathering around the story of Jesus to cement our commitment to his "way" of life. That is what is so encouraging and hopeful about the shift in which we find ourselves. It does not take us away from Jesus and his message. It challenges us to discard whatever prevents us from focusing on Jesus who gave such clear human expression to the Divine. It helps us to see and hear Jesus who reveals the truth of who we are as bearers of the Divine. It challenges us to commit ourselves to his dream for a better world.

It is our privilege to be "ecclesia", to know, celebrate and ritual-ize this "good news story" of ourselves and all humanity. We have a story to gather around that is affirming, uplifting, chal-lenging and hopeful. This is a story our world needs.

Let us raise our voices and proclaim it decisively and courageously.

More titles by Michael Morwood - available in paperback editions.

Tomorrow's Catholic. Understanding God and Jesus in a New Millennium 1997. USA edition: Twenty-Third Publications. Mystic, CT. Australian edition: Spectrum Publications, Richmond, Vic. Australia

I was reminded of a book that shook the foundations of Christianity back in 1963. *Honest to God*, by Anglican Bishop John A. T. Robinson was a radical work, radical in the sense that it got to the roots of belief and practice, unafraid to discuss the most sacrosanct, inviolable subjects. It was, like this book, a very readable small work, requiring no great theological mind to understand what the author was getting at. Modest as it was, it contained gems of wisdom that resonated beautifully with what many hearts were thinking at the time. *Tomorrow's Catholic* is another such gem that will not go unnoticed because it is meant for ordinary people, struggling to make sense of a religion increasingly out of touch with people's lives, beliefs, desires and expectations.

- Eugene H. Ciarlo, book editor for *The American Catholic*

Is Jesus God? Finding Our Faith. 2001 USA edition: Crossroad Publishing Company. NY. Australian edition: Spectrum Publications.

> A provocative, powerful and life-giving book! Michael Morwood is raising ... the right and obvious questions that all Christians must face. In his response he provides fresh and perceptive possibilities for a modern and relevant faith.
>
> - Bishop John Shelby Spong
>
> This is the book I have been waiting for...Everyone I know who has read this book appreciates its premise and applauds its author.
>
> - *National Catholic Reporter* review 10th August 2001

Praying a New Story. 2004 USA edition: Orbis Books, Maryknoll. NY.

Award Winner, Best Spiritual Books, *Spirituality & Health Awards 2004:*

> Invigorating, poetic and imaginative ... the perfect resource for small groups interested in exploring new avenues of devotion and spiritual practice.

From Sand to Solid Ground. Questions of Faith for Modern Christians. 2007. USA edition: Crossroad Publishing Company. NY.

The work responds to the need of contemporary Christians to understand their faith in a new way which respects their secular world-view and enables them to believe in Christ and believe in themselves and our place in the universe. Morwood's style is direct and challenging yet compassionate and reassuring. Christians who are looking for a 21st century handle for their faith will be rewarded by their effort to read this important work.

- *USA Catholic Press Awards 2008,* 3rd place: Education:

From Sand to Solid Ground is an extraordinary book of courage and vision. Michael Morwood dares to speak and articulate clearly what more and more Catholics today quietly struggle with and question. His writing exemplifies the giftedness of a true teacher. The book's simple yet elegant style succeeds where perhaps more scholarly, academic theology does not. True teaching not only exposes and explains but inspires and explores as well. Morwood's passionate approach to the faith does all of this and more.

- Barbara Fiand, author of *From Religion Back to Faith* and *In the Stillness You Will Know*:

Children Praying a New Story. A Resource for Parents, Grandparents and Teachers. 2009. Kelmor Publishing. South Bend. Indiana. Available from http://www.morwood.org Also available in electronic editions.

This is not a book for children. It is a resource for educators and for any adult Christian seeking to deepen understanding of faith in light of the "new story" of the universe and the development of life on earth. The book responds to adult questions such as: How do we now think about, understand or teach Christmas or Easter or Pentecost? How do we pray? How might we pray with young children at home or in a classroom? How can we use gospel stories about Jesus? How do "sacraments" fit into the new story?

> If you are a parent, grandparent or teacher our role is not to introduce our children, grandchildren or students into our faith or our parents' faith. As a sixty seven year old Liverpool-Irish-Canadian-Catholic the Catholic Church today is radically different from the church into which I was baptized over a font in St. James, Bootle, in 1942.
>
> It is a different church and a different faith for my children and hopefully for my grandchildren. Michael Morwood, in responding to the questions and faith struggles of adults, many of them parents, grandparents and teachers, has given us a way to introduce God and

Jesus to future generations for whom the new story is as familiar as multiplication tables were to us.

- John Quinn, Editor, *NewCatholicTimes,* Canada. October 19, 2009

God Is Near. Understanding a Changing Church. 1991. Australian edition. Spectrum Publications, Richmond, Vic. Australia, is no longer in print. USA edition, 2002, God Is Near: Trusting Our Faith, Crossroad Publishing Company. NY.

Faith, Hope and a Bird Called George. A Spiritual Fable. 2011 USA edition: Twenty-Third Publications, New London. Ct. Australian edition: John Garratt Publishing, Mulgrave. Vic.

For articles and other information:

http://www.morwood.org

Made in the USA
San Bernardino, CA
18 March 2017